De Benneville R. Keim

San Domingo

Pen pictures and leaves of travel, romance and history, from the portfolio of a correspondent in the American tropics

De Benneville R. Keim

San Domingo

Pen pictures and leaves of travel, romance and history, from the portfolio of a correspondent in the American tropics

ISBN/EAN: 9783337048792

Printed in Europe, USA, Canada, Australia, Japan

Cover: Foto ©Andreas Hilbeck / pixelio.de

More available books at **www.hansebooks.com**

SAN DOMINGO.

PEN PICTURES AND LEAVES OF TRAVEL, ROMANCE AND HISTO
FROM THE PORTFOLIO OF A CORRESPONDENT
IN THE AMERICAN TROPICS.

BY DeB. RANDOLPH KEIM,

AUTHOR OF SHERIDAN'S TROOPERS ON THE BORDERS.

PHILADELPHIA:
CLAXTON, REMSEN & HAFFELFINGER.
Nos. 819 & 821 MARKET STREET
1870.

Entered according to Act of Congress, in the year 1870, by

DE B. RANDOLPH KEIM,

In the Office of the Librarian of Congress, at Washington.

THIS VOLUME, WITH PERMISSION, IS MOST RESPECTFULLY DEDICATED TO

U. S. GRANT,

PRESIDENT OF THE UNITED STATES

AS AN HUMBLE RECOGNITION OF HIS PATRIOTISM AND STATESMANSHIP

IN SEEKING TO

PROMOTE THE DIGNITY AND GREATNESS OF HIS COUNTRY BY THE ESTABLISHMENT OF

AMERICAN SUPREMACY ON AMERICAN SOIL.

PREFACE.

THE lack of information of late date, and the entire absence of recent works respecting the island of San Domingo, have led the author to believe that a small volume on that subject might be timely and useful. In the summer of 1869, the author visited San Domingo in search of practical knowledge to be spread before the numerous readers of THE HERALD. During his brief sojourn, through the assistance of many valuable and distinguished acquaintances, he was enabled to become familiar with the affairs of the island. Among those to whom he feels particularly indebted may be mentioned Bueneventura Baez, President of the Republic, Jose Hungria, M. M. Gautier, Felix Del Monte, Ricardo Curiel, Ministers of the various departments of the Government, Senor Leyba, J. Somers Smith, United States Commercial Agent, and Eugene P. Smith. Having visited the magnificent Bay of Samana, the author made the journey from Puerto Plata, on the north coast, to the capital of the

Republic on the south, viewing the finest features of all the bewildering charms presented by the face of nature.

Aside from an unparalleled diversity of landscape, an extraordinary fecundity of soil, rivers and mountains opulent in the precious and the grosser metals, and forests teeming with vegetable productions of great value and abundance, San Domingo is also a land of romance and eventful history. The author intends not to be deprived, in the routine of a traveler's narrative, of the benefit of many pleasant episodes, and therefore has interwoven in the thread of his story much which may appear digressive, and may occasion the imputation of wandering.

The author has only to add that his own time in visiting the island was one of the pleasantest experiences of a long list of extensive and distant journeys, and he only hopes that the reader may derive as much pleasure in this reproduction of that experience as the author did in securing it.

WASHINGTON, D. C., 1870.

CONTENTS.

CHAPTER I.
AN INTRODUCTORY SCRAP OF HISTORY - - 13

CHAPTER II.
LAND TO THE "STARBOARD"—A TRAVELER'S IMPRESSIONS—ARRIVAL IN THE OZAMA—POPULAR DEMONSTRATIONS - - - - 17

CHAPTER III.
THE CUSTOM-HOUSE—INLAND COMMERCE—A BUSY SCENE—THE "CERCLE DU COMMERCE" - 25

CHAPTER IV.
A DINNER ON SHORE—A REGULAR BOARDER—A DISCUSSION - - - - - - 30

CHAPTER V.
A STROLL IN THE CITY—THE STREETS—BUILDINGS—HISTORICAL NOTES—THE WALLS - - 37

CHAPTER VI.
THE STORY OF MIGUEL DIAZ AND ZAMEACA - 47

CONTENTS.

CHAPTER VII.
THE OCCUPATION OF THE HAYNA—FOUNDING OF SAN DOMINGO - - - - - 53

CHAPTER VIII.
A VISIT TO THE PRESIDENT OF THE REPUBLIC—THE CABINET - - - - 61

CHAPTER IX.
AN INTERVIEW - - - - - 67

CHAPTER X.
EXCURSION TO THE CAVES OF SANTA ANNA - 77

CHAPTER XI.
CELEBRATION OF THE FESTIVAL OF CORPUS CHRISTI—A THEATRICAL PERFORMANCE - - 84

CHAPTER XII.
OFF FOR SAMANA—THE DOMINICAN FLEET IN TOW—A NAVAL ENGAGEMENT - - 91

CHAPTER XIII.
SAMANA BAY—ITS PHYSICAL FEATURES—THE PENINSULA—NOTES OF HISTORY - - - 100

CHAPTER XIV.
SAMANA BAY AND THE WARS IN THE ANTILLES - 112

CHAPTER XV.
NEGOTIATIONS OF THE UNITED STATES FOR THE ACQUISITION OF SAMANA - - - - 118

CHAPTER XVI.

COTABANAMA, THE GIANT KING - - - 129

CHAPTER XVII.

ARRIVAL AT PUERTO PLATA—THE GOVERNOR OF
THE CITY—FAREWELL TO THE TYBEE—OFF
FOR THE INTERIOR - - - - - 135

CHAPTER XVIII.

TRAVELING UNDER DIFFICULTIES—AN UNIQUE
ESTABLISHMENT—A MOTLEY RETINUE—AS-
CENDING THE MONTE CHRISTI RANGE—SCENES
ON THE ROAD - - - - - - 143

CHAPTER XIX.

A HARD DAY'S JOURNEY—BAD ROADS—HOSPI-
TALITY—A FEAST—THE WIDOW OF AN AMERI-
CAN NEGRO - - - - - - 150

CHAPTER XX.

A NATIVE FARM—ONCE MORE ON THE ROAD—
ARRIVAL AT SANTIAGO DE LOS CABALLEROS—
SEÑOR JOSÉ M. GLAS—HOSPITALITY—THE CITY
—A MASONIC CELEBRATION - - - - 160

CHAPTER XXI.

CAONABO, CHIEF OF THE CIBAO - - - 169

CHAPTER XXII.

THE PERPLEXITIES OF TRAVEL—AN UNTIMELY
JOLLIFICATION—A NOCTURNAL INTERRUPTION
—TWO UNPROTECTED FEMALES - - - 180

CHAPTER XXIII.

CHARMING SCENERY—LA VEGA REAL—THE TOWN OF LA VEGA—HOSPITALITIES - - - 190

CHAPTER XXIV.

CROSSING LA VEGA REAL—UNPARALLELED BEAUTY OF LANDSCAPE—GRAZING HERDS—CROSSING THE YUNA—COTUY—CAMP IN THE MOUNTAINS - - - - - - - 197

CHAPTER XXV.

AN UMBRELLA AS AN EXPEDIENT IN A STORM—A TROPICAL SUNRISE—A FORAGING EXPEDITION—CROSSING THE OZAMA—LESSONS IN NATATION—THE ISABELLA—A NOVEL MODE OF FERRYING—ARRIVAL AT THE CITY GATE AFTER HOURS - - - - - 207

CHAPTER XXVI.

REFLECTIONS ON MY JOURNEY—A NOVEL METHOD OF GETTING RID OF MY SERVANT AND PEON—PLACES AND SUBJECTS OF INTEREST IN THE CAPITAL—THE CHURCH—THE CATHEDRAL—COLUMBUS' REMAINS - - - - - 220

CHAPTER XXVII.

THE CONVENT OF SAN FRANCISCO—ALONZO DE DE OJEDA - - - - - - - 233

CHAPTER XXVIII.

THE STORY OF ALONZO DE OJEDA—CONTINUED - 243

CONTENTS.

CHAPTER XXXVII.
THE GOVERNMENT—MILITARY AND NAVAL FORCE 327

APPENDIX - - - - - - 333

SAN DOMINGO.

CHAPTER I.

AN INTRODUCTORY SCRAP OF HISTORY.

THE daring Genoese, amazed and perplexed at the marvelous discoveries constantly unfolding before him, was in doubt whither to direct the course of his little fleet. Having safely steered through the unknown and dangerous channels of the Bahamas, he reached the island of Cuba. Dazzled by the opening of a new world, the simplest utterances of the innocent natives were construed into the most impossible fancies. The rude sailing chart of Toscanelli was consulted, and distorted by pliant imaginations into any shape that might suit the bewildered reasoning of the discoverers. The theories of this grave authority were confirmed, for, in their credulous state of mind, Columbus and his companions were ready and willing to console all differences, however great or inconsistent.

To add to his doubts, Columbus now determined that Cuba was not the famed island of Cipango, but that it was the mainland of Asia, and that he was not far from Mangi and Cathay. Discouraged, at the moment of solving the mystery of the land that lay before him he turned back in his course.

He was now more than ever perplexed. During this moment of indecision, Columbus set his caravals before the wind. While pondering over his vague thoughts and speculations, a new vision confronted his astonished gaze. Before him rose great mountains. The salubrity of the climate had already arrested his attention; but the bold peaks of Hayti portrayed through the bright atmosphere upon the blue canvas of the heavens were enchanting. As he approached the land, a bold iron-bound coast, beautiful savannas and the distant Cordilleras of the Cibao opened in delightful detail. His eyes had not yet rested upon such surpassing majesty of nature. The charming scenery and the birds reminded him of Andalusia. Overpowered with enthusiasm, he named the country Hispaniola in honor of the land of his adoption. A fort was built on the western end of the island, and as an act of patriotic piety, Columbus erected a cross in honor of the spread of the boundaries of religion, and the extension of the dominions of Castile and Leon.

Leaving Diego de Arana, of Cordova, notary and alguazil to the Armament, with thirty-nine men, early in January Columbus turned his prow homeward. After a few days' sail he espied a beautiful headland which he named Capo del Enamorado, or Lover's Cape, now Cape Cabron. A spacious bay, surrounded by high mountains, covered with towering forests of mahogany, dawned upon him. Charmed with the prospect, the little fleet entered, and tarried for several days. In commemoration of an unfortunate occurrence with the natives, Columbus gave the bay the name El Golfo de las Flechas, the Gulf of Arrows. It is now known as the Bay of Samana, while but a portion still bears the appropriate and historic designation given by Columbus.

Such is the opening page of the History of San Domingo. The traveler of to-day, as he gazes upon the bold coast of that matchless island, wonders not at the boundless surprise of Columbus. After the perils of a protracted voyage across a trackless and unknown ocean; influenced by all the superstitions of the age; thrown into fearful doubt and uncertainty by the strange and terrible notions entertained by the scientific men of the day respecting the configuration of the earth, the undertaking was doubly bold and hazardous.

The timid ventures along the coast of Africa or to the Azores, had hitherto constituted the acme of nautical skill and enterprise. Although the cosmography of the day had led him into many errors respecting the nature and situation of the countries he had discovered, he had broken through the limits of human knowledge. He had extended the boundaries of civilization and christianity. To maritime enterprise he had given a new field. He had contributed the key which opened a new domain in the realms of geographical science. More than all, he had triumphed in an undertaking that had cost him years of toil and sneers, anxiety and importunity. He had repaid his patron Queen with a new world.

CHAPTER II.

LAND TO THE "STARBOARD"—A TRAVELER'S IMPRESSIONS—ARRIVAL IN THE OZAMA—POPULAR DEMONSTRATIONS.

AT eight o'clock on the morning of June 17, 1869, the steamer Tybee, Delanoy, master, bore in sight of the island of San Domingo. A low coast line, covered to the very edge of the tidal waves with a profuse vegetation, skirted the ocean. Inland rose the bold summits of the southern mountain ranges, at first like so many dark leaden clouds portending a storm, but upon a closer approach, bursting forth in all their grandeur of forest and color. We had now fairly entered the tropical latitudes. The tremulous atmosphere was laden with the fragrance of the land. The blue waters beneath were tranquil, broken only by innumerable spray-tipped ripples, stretching far off into the hazy horizon. Innumerable flying fish sported about, their gracefully poised movements affording a field for speculation upon aerial locomotion. Numerous land and sea birds flirted in the air. The good ship ploughed her course bravely through the liquid highway, and fast lessened the "knots" on the line of her voyage.

The passengers, besides myself, and not more than six in number, had gathered about the captain's cabin, in eager anxiety to catch the first glimpse of the land-marks of port. As on all similar occasions, the captain was bustling about, with one eye on the compass and the other ranging the horizon through a ponderous and sea-stained spy-glass.

Delanoy was a genial, jolly old "skipper," whose lifetime of sea-faring, strange to say, had served to develop his better qualities. He had always on hand a good story or a joke, and at times rose into the higher sphere of nautical romance, that might do to tell to the marines. In the midst of his anxiety, looking out for a strange harbor, in a strange sea, he good-naturedly took the endless interrogatories put to him, and not unfrequently relieved himself of a short yarn, by way of celebrating a speedy turn in port.

Among our passengers was an itinerary American diplomat, who having served his country in the consular service, and figured in several prominent enterprises under the "Empire" in Mexico, was now plying his task in the way of securing concessions from the Baez government in San Domingo. Diplomatically considered, the gentleman had one peculiarity which highly fitted him for his duties; that was extreme deafness—quite a convenience for confidential consultation. It was said at opportune times his tympanum became quite sensitive; also a singular fact which much puzzled the brains of the unsophisticated. In the same connection, it was also added that the gentleman heard a great deal more than he got credit for, and with equal flexibility did not hear a great many things that were not appropriate nor desirable to hear. Another passenger carried great financial schemes in his brain, and a very broad-brimmed hat on his head. A representative of the owners of the ship; the gentleman's wife; an individual I could not precisely assort; a young man who indulged in a blessed appetite for food and slumber, and myself, composed the balance.

An hour before noon, we ranged in sight of the three lofty spires of the Sierra Gorda range of mountains, set down in the "skipper's" navigator's guide as covering the port of San Domingo. The appearance of these unmistakable land-marks was hailed with a sigh of relief by the indefatigable Delanoy, and certainly was not an unpleasant prospect of *terra firma* to those accustomed to more substantial footing than the deck of a ship.

Every eye was now turned towards the three solitary peaks, gradually expanding in view. Every moment a new scene opened, until not only the mountain range was quite distinctly visible, distantly inland, but the city of San Domingo itself, with its ancient towers and bastions, its gray walls, its vine covered ruins, its antique dwellings, its clusters of cocoanut, banana, and palm, suddenly broke in upon the vision.

By noon the steamer "opened" the mouth of the Ozama, upon the west bank of which the city was built. There was a great commotion on shore. It was evidently a matter of uncertainty as to the Tybee's true character, this being her first voyage, and the object of her mission being a mystery. It was no wonder. A few days before, the pirate Telegrafo, belonging to Lupernon, one of the revolutionists, appeared off Puerto Plata under a strange flag, and fired upon the city. It was not known but that we might be the Telegrafo, on a visit to pay the same courtesy of a little iron and gunpowder, by way of communication with the capital of the Republic.

From the shore the beating of drums could be heard, followed by the mustering of troops in the batteries ranging upon us. The people, old and young, flocked in convenient and protected places to see what was going on. A signal gun at this juncture from the Tybee might have called from the gathering population a *pronunciamiento*. But the Tybee fired no gun, and the people made no *pronunciamiento*. Aft we flew the American colors, and, at the fore and mizzen, the jack and owners' signal.

Until something were known to the contrary, the flag protected us, but the precautions on shore were certainly wise, in order to prevent surprise. The pilot evidently had made up his mind not to fall into a trap, if he could help it. He studiously kept within convenient retreating distance of the shore, allowing the steamer to come in. Slowing up, the Tybee headed directly for the mouth of the river. When within a hundred yards of the shore, the pilot, a burly mulatto, in a pair of dirty cotton breeches, formerly white, a blue check shirt with one button, a straw hat and bare feet, climbed up the ship's "side." As he stepped on deck he gave a furtive glance from one side to the other, surveying the groups of passengers and sailors gathered around. He must have been satisfied that there was nothing *revolutionary* about that craft, for he followed up the satisfactory discovery of a genuine and strange American steamer for port with a volley of salutations in Spanish.

Whether the pilot was more pleased at the agreeable visit which awaited his anxious countrymen on shore, or rejoiced most at the prospect of a rich fee, will have to remain undetermined. Suffice it to say, that he paced the deck and gave orders to the men at the helm with the dignity and self-satisfaction of an admiral. When the pilot came aboard the Dominican flag was hoisted at the main. This put an end to the suspense on shore. The people came out from their hiding-places, and now crowded upon the parapets, shouting lustily and waving divers fabrics and extremities of garments with a gusto that showed a spontaneous explosion of welcome and good-feeling.

As the Tybee steamed inside the heads of the Ozama, she let off a salute of one gun, from an old-fashioned piece of metal, which looked as if it had belonged to the epoch of the buccaneers. The sailors had rammed the cannon, for I believe it was formerly classified under that head, about half full of tow, in addition to an extra allowance of gunpowder. The deafening detonations aroused a number of aquatic birds in the vicinity, which, not accustomed to such a violent disturbance of the quiet atmosphere overhanging the Ozama, set up a distracting confusion of shrill sounds. The people from the shore responded by yelling more vigorously. The enthusiasm of the moment was heightened by a return of the salute from one of the batteries of the city. As we entered the river, on the "port side" stood a venerable structure, a tower dating back to the days of Columbus, and following the banks of the stream were the walls and battlements on the river front. On the "starboard" side the country extended for some distance in a level plain, about twenty feet above the river, and covered with trees and undergrowth in all the rich luxuriance of the tropics.

The steamer proceeded about a quarter of a mile up the river, and moored against the custom-house dock. As soon as we made fast, the custom-house officers came aboard, one remaining during our entire stay in port.

The Ozama, for vessels of great draft, is entirely unsuitable, in consequence of insufficiency of water. Large vessels are obliged to anchor outside, in the roads in front of the city, which lie off about three-quarters of a mile. The roads are open to all winds from the south, southeast, half east, southwest, and west, and in a sea breeze to the southward there is a heavy swell. The bottom is of black sand and mud, with good holding ground. Within a mile of the signal tower on the west point of the mouth of the river, the soundings range from forty to fifty fathoms, diminishing towards the shore to ten fathoms, and thence gradually shallowing to the beach. The east point of the entrance is flat and rocky. The river inside is a safe and excellent harbor, but across its mouth extends a solid rock, with never more than thirteen and a half feet of water. The width of the river is not over one hundred yards.

CHAPTER III.

THE CUSTOM-HOUSE—INLAND COMMERCE—A BUSY SCENE—THE "CERCLE DU COMMERCE."

HE arrival of the Tybee was the sensation of the day, and as the quiet community, vegetating within the walls of the capital of the Republic were not often disturbed by external excitements of this nature, this one created particular enthusiasm. The custom-house consisted of a row of one-story stone buildings, plastered and white-washed on the exterior. A shelter for the protection of merchandise being unladen, stood upon the open space between the buildings and the rude dock. A high wooden fence formed the enclosure on the side leading towards the only gate in the eastern wall.

In the opposite direction, higher up the stream, was the landing-place of the passengers and dug-outs of the natives, bringing the productions from the country above. Also large quantities of logwood in rafts were floated down and landed at the same place.

Every morning the scene on the river and on the shore was very animated. From the earliest dawn a constant stream of small craft, the majority resembling what in the United States would be called canoes, and occasionally a dilapidated ship's launch, might be seen rounding the bend in the river, and paddling or drifting down to the landing, just above the steamer. Each canoe was managed by a man and a woman, two men, or a man and a boy, but always in twos. The boats were loaded to the water's edge with every variety of tropical fruit, vegetables, roots, and green blades of corn-stalks for horse-feed, also tobacco, sugar, coffee, and cotton, in small quantities. The bulk of the boats I observed were more largely laden with bananas and plantains, the staple food of the country.

This freight was discharged and deposited upon mats spread on the river bank. Here the retail dealers came to replenish their stocks. Such a chattering and bargaining would have done justice to an oriental market scene. From the deck of the steamer, while enjoying the freshness of the morning air, this sight was one of particular amusement. I discovered that the old women were the best on a sale, and generally the men withdrew in their favor when an especially obdurate or threatening customer put in an appearance.

A short time after day-light the whole space from the city walls to the river bank, covering an area of more than an acre, in that particular spot, was thronged with men, women and children, donkeys, and bullocks, on the one hand, and men, women, boys, and girls, and their articles for sale, on the other. For hours, indeed during the entire day, but principally in the morning, a constant stream of human beings, beasts of burden, and carts were pouring into the city, and others were pouring out, on their way to the landing to renew their supplies.

As a general thing these business transactions were conducted peaceably, though at times a row would take place, when the rival combatants would draw their *machetas* and flourish them at each other. I do not remember ever seeing any blood spilt, or so much as even coming to blows. The fine art of a fistic adjustment of disputes is unknown. The white, black, and mulatto, descendants of the Spaniards, now inhabiting the island, inherit true Castilian readiness to use the *machete*, and with this arrange all their controversies that cannot otherwise be brought into harmony very speedily and with very little explanation.

The first person on board the steamer, after the custom-house officer, was the proprietor of the "Cercle du Commerce," the only hotel in the city, and kept by a Frenchman, known, by way of abbreviation, as Auguste. P. Soulie signed all bills—I believe the two were the same. Auguste was a robust Frenchman, and, judging from his healthy exterior, tropical climate and mode of life agreed with him. Withal he was an excellent recommendation of the good cheer of his hotel.

Auguste, French like, was very obsequious. The gingle of American eagles was, to his ears, more musical than the rustle of Dominican shin-plasters. I was afterwards informed that the Frenchman had made an effort to entertain Dominicans at his hotel, but that they forgot to settle up, or could not settle up, or, when they did settle up, the compensation amounted to no more than so much waste paper; that the debit side of the hotel accounts grew wonderfully, until the weight of liabilities completely crushed the meagre assets, and, beneath the pressure of this preponderance, came a crash.

Auguste, profiting by this experience, as well as opportunity, shut his doors upon native patronage, and sought only the favors of strangers. This he found not only lucrative—for a traveler's vanity to parade his liberality kept Auguste's wine cellar in a constant stir of activity—but he once more found himself on his feet.

The special object of Auguste's visit to the steamer was to verbally announce the existence of a hotel in the city, and that he was the proprietor, and would like to learn how many would be on shore that afternoon, so that he might know " how much dinner to get."

As we were craving for a change from steamer fare and a little stretch on *terra firma*, the Frenchman was bewildered and made happy by receiving in reply that we would all be to dinner that evening at six o'clock.

Rejoicing in the prospect, Mons. Auguste hastened over the side of the vessel, and darted homeward, to throw open the portals of the "Cercle du Commerce." At three o'clock in the afternoon, our party made an exodus from the steamer. As there was some time before the hour fixed for dinner, we entered within the walls of the city by the Ataranza gate, and took occasion to parade the narrow streets, by way of an opening flourish of acquaintance with the capital of the Dominican Republic.

CHAPTER IV.

A DINNER ON SHORE—A REGULAR BOARDER— A DISCUSSION.

AT six o'clock, our party, eight in number, seated themselves at Mons. Auguste's bounteous board. Our number was further increased by a regular boarder, a Frenchman, a crusty, cranky bachelor, who had long lived in the tropics—that is, in Mexico. The gentleman revelled in the dignity and importance of the rank of Consul, having held that position for years at Tampico, I believe, and was merely at San Domingo to relieve the regular Consul while on a lengthy leave of absence to *La Belle France*. His anxiety to get back to his regular post, and the protracted absence of the permanent official, did not set well upon the mind and conscience of our consular celibate, so that a naturally crotchetty temperament was rendered doubly crotchetty and annoying by this invasion of official life at Tampico.

The hotel was an antique, capacious structure, built after the style of architecture in vogue in Spanish countries several centuries ago. The walls were thick and of stone; the roof was flat and tiled with red clay tiles; the floors, on the *rez de chaussée*, were stone. The dining-room was high, airy, and spacious. The furniture was simple. The bare, coarsely plastered, and white-washed walls, by way of giving vent to the natural patriotic zeal of his countrymen, were decorated with an assortment of steel engravings of French heroes of the Napoleon wars, and scenes during that eventful period.

The dining-table was spread after the fashion of the French, with merely the service. An immaculate table-cloth, and china and glass, in the same condition, were not only inviting to appetites about to enjoy a change of fare, but suggested thrift and good living as a natural consequence.

Our dinner, like all other similar occasions had its courses, from soup, through the various stages of the acknowleged routine, down to the dessert, which, in this particular instance, consisted of a variety of the fruits of the country. Considerable interest and curiosity was here manifested. Fruits never before heard of, much less tasted, were experimented upon with various results, which clearly indicated that all palates, like other things in nature, were not alike. This feature of the dinner was characteristically French and certainly very appropriate. Oranges, pine-apples, rose-apples, sapotas, the Avocado pear, mangoes, and excellent bananas were brought on in the greatest profusion, and disposed of with divers observations as to their respective merits. I had tasted some of the finest fruits of tropical Asia, but put in my voice in favor of the fruits of San Domingo, in variety, luscious flavor, and delicate fibre.

I had almost overlooked a novel dish which formed part of one of the regular courses. It was the palm cabbage. On the island there are several species of palm. The palmetto royal, (*Areca Oleracea,*) has at its utmost summit, shooting above and from the centre of its clusters of immense, graceful, drooping fan-like leaves, a green top. This is what is known as the mountain, or palm cabbage. It grows in layers, concentrically arranged, and is of a rich cream-color. It is cut and prepared as our own lettuce.

During the dessert, Mons. Auguste replaced the inevitable Julien with Cognac and San Domingo rum, the latter a native production and of fair quality. The choicest vintage of France, was also periodically exhumed from Auguste's cellar. The finest brands of the Dominican "weed" were indulged with all the satisfaction of the best Havanas, which in truth they equalled.

At the later stages of the dinner, Señor Curiel, Secretary of the Treasury, and Señor Leyba, a prominent merchant, joined our party. Mons. Auguste was now upon the towering summit of his pride and importance. He stood at the head of the table with the air of one who had accomplished a great feat, and was just halting for a moment to enjoy his triumph.

The hours rolled quickly by. Our diplomatic friend had materially recovered his hearing and was entertaining everybody with remarkable vivacity. The sea-faring Delanoy dropped in a *dry* joke or two, at timely moments, which essentially aided the action of the risible muscles. Our consular friend, my *vis-à-vis* at the table, pounced upon me as the outlet of a large amount of spleen. Whether his own physical and mental discrepancies, or whether our intrusion upon the late quiet of the hotel was the cause, I am unable to say, but it was sufficient to know that his consular dignity was in rather a topsy-turvy condition, and I was the butt of all information he had to communicate on a diversity of subjects.

Having poured off another copious supply of "Dominican," as a settler to several others which preceded, the Frenchman said that the United States Government wanted to absorb all the West Indies. I said that the destiny of all the countries on the Western Hemisphere was disenthrallment from foreign rule. He said, "What do you mean?" I said I meant that England and France would have but little hold upon the soil of America in a few years. He said France would never haul down her flag where it had once been planted. I said, interrogatively and mildly, How about Mexico?

At this period in the dialogue, which had been on the part of the consul, somewhat heated, either by Dominican rum, or effervescing ire, my friend halted in his conversation for a few expletives, *à la Française*, which his pent up rage now would no longer restrain. His soliloquy was barely audible, and certainly not comprehensible.

At this exhibition of himself, the consular functionary seemed to be entirely oblivious; but Mons. Auguste, who was of a passive temperament, was by no means an indifferent spectator of the obstreperous behaviour of his countryman. For my own benefit, he would drop in, by way of parenthesis, a conciliatory observation not altogether favorable to the consul. That individual would at times look at Mons. Auguste, who, upon seeing the official head turning that way, would hastily cast an admiring and studious gaze upon the ceiling, as the most convenient diversion.

My French friend, however, was not to be so easily put down; so renewing his familiarities with "Dominican," he launched out in a tirade against American institutions and everything American. As no one was now paying attention, except, perhaps, the landlord, American institutions accordingly suffered. The Frenchman grew disgusted with the lack of defference to his views and importance, and left the table, probably greatly to his own relief.

The first visit on shore passed off well, and the initiation into Dominican customs was favorable. Everyone congratulated Mons. Auguste upon his success in the dinner; all of which was in turn diplomatically and with well-feigned modesty heartily abused by the apologies of Mons. Auguste.

Towards ten o'clock, our party broke up, and a portion, myself among the number, set out for the steamer. The first thing after leaving the hotel, was a patrol shouting in front of us, at a distance of fifty yards, "*Quien viva.*" In response to this challenge, we informed the individual that we were Americans, whereupon we were permitted to pass. This sort of nocturnal salutation is very common in the capital of the Republic, as I subsequently discovered. On the present occasion, we were overhauled at least a half dozen times in going no greater distance than a quarter of a mile. When we reached the Ataranza gate, we were without the key, and had to send back to the officer on duty at the barracks for that influential instrument in removing the obstructions in our way.

After a delay of some minutes, a small door within the gate was opened and we were permitted to pass out, greatly to our relief, and the speedy prospects of a good night's rest on board the steamer.

CHAPTER V.

A STROLL IN THE CITY—THE STREETS—BUILDINGS—
HISTORICAL NOTES—THE WALLS.

ON the steamer everything was activity—taking in an assorted cargo of the exports of the island, chiefly sugar, logwood, and mahogany. To revive in the mind the early historic associations, dating back to the days of Columbus, or to receive the courtesies of newly made and attentive friends, was an agreeable diversion on shore.

The next afternoon I left the steamer for a second stroll through the city. Entering by the Ataranza gate, I directed my steps through some of the principal streets. San Domingo I found, in every respect, a Spanish city. Having been laid out and mostly, in fact completely, built, as regarded its area, in the days of the Columbuses and their immediate successors, the city possessed all the peculiarities of that remote period. The streets were extremely narrow, not more than eighteen to twenty feet in width, with a side-walk on either side of not more than three feet. The streets were covered with a hard cement, were smooth, and generally well preserved. They answered for man, beast, and vehicles promiscuously.

The buildings in the heart of the city were, generally, substantial. Those that bore the traces of antiquity, were constructed of limestone. Many of the more modern were built of a composition of earth, gravel, and a cement called "tapia." I was informed the process of putting up a building of this kind was, first to construct pillars, or station upright beams, and then erect a temporary boarding inside and outside, and fill this mould with "tapia." After this became hard, the boards were removed and the walls, strengthened by the stone pillars or wooden beams, became solid and durable.

The larger houses were built on a square with an inner quadrangle. The windows were high up from the ground, above the line of vision of ordinary specimens of the human family. The windows were noticibly large, probably for the admission of plenty of air, and in place of glass, or shutters, were protected by iron rods, forming a sort of basket in front. The doors were decidedly antique, and were made heavy enough for a prison gate, or sufficiently wide and high to answer for a carriage-drive.

The buildings all had flat tiled roofs, and the majority, indeed all in the heart of the city, were two stories in height. Judging from the looks of these structures, the most of them were the same built originally upon the site. As a rule the residences were exceedingly plain in their exterior appearance. A few were embellished about the windows, over the doors and under the eaves, with those peculiar designs of chiseling and ornamentation, so frequently met in ancient Spanish structures. It was very evident, from the moss and mould that had accumulated to hide these attempts at architectural elegance, that these buildings were not of recent date, but must have been reared and occupied by some successful adventurer, on the sea or land, during the palmiest days of "Domingo."

A few of the streets were devoted to shops, that is business there monopolized the larger share of the buildings, though with the exception of those facing on the market-place, there was no portion of the city entirely given up to this purpose. Here the retail shops and small dealers had gathered. The wholesale houses and importers were nearer the heart of the city. The consulates and steamship offices occupied no particular locality. During the presence of the steamer in port the American flag was constantly flying, and by this ensign, it was not difficult to find this spot, which by the enlightenment of the age, was for the time being invested with all the nationality and dignity of American soil.

Approaching the walls of the city, the habitations dwindled down to small hovels, or wooden structures, built of upright posts driven into the ground and roofed over with a thick thatch made out of banana leaves.

San Domingo is to-day the oldest living European city on the Western Hemisphere, and with all its facilities and past opportunities should have been the metropolis of the western tropical world. The city was founded in 1494. The original settlement stood on the eastern bank of the Ozama, and was called La Nueva Isabella, In 1502, this town was destroyed by a hurricane. The present city was then built upon the west bank and received its new name. It is said that it was called after the father of Columbus. This statement, however, I have been unable to verify any further than to have been told so by a priest, and also to have seen it stated in a work without giving the authority. I do not contradict the assertion, but give it as I received it.

It would seem that the name was after San Domingo, a canonized personage, who figures at the head of the pious concourse of patron saints of Castile.

San Domingo is a walled city, with bastions and citadels, such as was at the time the custom in building what might be called military cities. The plan—that is its walls, form a trapezoid, the northwest angle being cut off. The principal streets are laid out at right angles, running a little west of north and north of east. From the Archiepiscopal Palace to the Bastion of La Conception, a street runs diagonally across the entire width of the city, making a sharp angle at the chapel of San Nicholas.

As I had still some time left before the hour fixed by Mons. Auguste for a renewal of his exhibitions in culinary tactics, I determined to take a walk around the city on the walls, a distance, I should judge, of over two miles. As I was at the time nearest the Bastion of La Conception, on the western side, I scrambled up a sodded embankment to the level space formerly designed for the defenders to stand upon, but now apparently much used by pedestrians. This bastion guarded one of the two main gates of the city, and covered three roads converging at this point. It overlooked an open country, and controlled an extensive sweep. The gates, as well as the bastion, were defended on the exterior by a moat and lunettes, but now in ruins. A strong guard was constantly on duty, with a commissioned officer, responsible to the military governor of the city, for every person who entered or departed. At eight o'clock in the evening the gates were closed, and no persons were allowed to pass until they were again opened, after daylight, the following morning.

I followed the walls the entire northwestern side of the city, until passing the Bastion San Antonio. Here, at the Bastion of Santa Barbara, the walls made an angle, running almost due east and west. This bastion occupied the crest of a prominent knoll, and was the key to the position. The view from here over the city, and out upon the broad blue ocean, was very fine.

A very short walk brought me to the extreme point of the walls touching upon the river. Here they made a sharp angle, taking a general south and north direction, but following the irregularities of the Ozama river, and in places close upon the margin, and again withdrew about fifty yards, except at two or three points, where the space in front was greater.

I continued my saunterings, and indulged in a delightful prospect of the river. Near by, on the outside, I passed the custom-house, and over the arches of the Ataranza gate, where there was a guard, and reached the Bastion Don Diego. This work jutted out upon the river, almost overhanging it. The high walls, and bold open embrasures, evidently marked this out as the principal inner stronghold, defending the river.

At the extreme end of the walls, on this side, I arrived at the point of land, bounded on one side by the entrance to the Ozama, and washed on the other by the waters of the ocean. The signal tower, the citadel, the barracks, and arsenal, all here occupy a large enclosure. The best effort of the engineers was bestowed upon this portion of the walls, commanding, as they did, the ocean approach and mouth of the river. I tarried very little time here, as I proposed subsequently visiting all the points of interest in the city in detail.

I now strolled down the ocean front. What a beautiful yet painful prospect! The same waters upon whose bosom floated the caravels of Columbus, the ancient treasure-laden ships, or the arriving vessels of the numerous adventurers from the old world, rolled there still. What associations of a thrilling past! What recollections of the startling deeds of the inimitable heroes of the then unknown and unexplored waste of waters! What a period of romantic exploits and daring achievement! It was from here sailed many of the expeditions that gave to the crown of Spain the dominion of continents and empires. It was from here that the majority of indomitable spirits of that age of maritime enterprise set out upon their perilous voyages, or returned to rest from a career of suffering and disappointment. Standing on such hallowed ground, with such a bewildering maze of history continually welling up in the mind, the head instinctively bowed in reverence to the everlasting ocean. Even the perishable surroundings became invested with a sanctity which inspired a feeling of due homage.

To-day all this activity and romance have vanished. With the exception of a schooner now and then beating into the river with an assorted cargo to supply the few wants of the simple people, or departing freighted with the valuable productions of nature, or again, the monthly mail steamer, and all is quiet and inert, as if the enterprise and industry of two centuries, while it lasted, had only reared here for themselves a monument to remind the living present of the zeal and prosperity of the dead and departed past.

I paused for a moment at the Bastions San Fernando and San José, and took a transient look at the iron frame-work of the tower, meant for a light-house to warn mariners of the dangerous coral reefs that lie along the coast, or to point out the entrance to the river.

I next reached the Bastion San Gil, at the southern angle of the walls. A short walk brought me back to my starting point, where I once more returned to the street, and hastily set out for the dinner table of Mons. Auguste.

The walls of San Domingo do not vary from those of the old walled cities of Europe, still met with where the invading hand of time and modern science have not obliterated all vestiges of the past. The walls averaged from nine to twelve feet in thickness and were built of stone, mostly stuccoed. They extended about a thousand yards along the Ozama, and very nearly that distance along the ocean front. At brief intervals sentry stations, or guard posts, were met with between the bastions. These bastions were intended for batteries of from four to eight guns. The walls, in many places, showed signs of neglect and decay, and were overgrown with vines. If they did not inspire an idea of life and activity, they certainly excited an admiration of picturesque effect. The walls varied in height. On the land and river sides they were from twelve to twenty-five feet, according to the configuration of the ground. On the ocean front they were not more than four feet, with embrasures at short intervals. The walls were entirely dismantled and unguarded, except at the Bastions La Conception, the Ataranza gate, and the citadel and barracks. Here on the point was a battery of old French guns, cast in the days of the Louis, and the oddest specimens of ordnance that I had ever seen, except the souvenirs of by-gone days of strife and victory to be found in our own navy-yards and arsenals. Indeed, everything had the appearance of a government debilitated by external and internal discord; paralyzed by lack of the spirit or the ability to rise; a land with a soil and climate capable of the highest production, and mountains laden with untold auriferous treasures, crushed by the evils of social and political disorganization, ignorance, profitless opposition to restraint, and, as a consequence, indifference in the inhabitants to all that envelopes a state in the surroundings of health and strength, and brings the rewards of happiness and affluence.

CHAPTER VI.

THE STORY OF MIGUEL DIAZ AND ZAMEACA.

UPON the banks of the beautiful river which now perpetuates the name of the primitive inhabitants, dwelt the Ozamas, a harmless, inoffensive and quiet people. The presence of a strange race, differing in color, stature and temperament, upon the north side of the island, was unknown, or at least had not yet been heard of more than through the vague stories passed by a hundred mouths.

Thoughtless other than of their immediate necessities, these happy people lived in blissful unconcern. In the solitudes of their sacred palm groves they performed their religious ceremonies. Bountiful nature provided for their wants with a lavish hand. They lived but to enjoy the favors which spread around them, demanding only the effort to gather.

The quiet river coursing in front of their frail habitations, was charming beyond description. Its banks were lined with overhanging trees and flowers.

Nothing could have been added to increase the beauty of scenery, the abundance of everything necessary to support life, or to improve that state of contentment, in which all the cultivation that elevates the human soul above its rudest type, is entirely unknown.

At the time of which we speak, the Ozamas were governed by a maiden cacique, Zameaca, or Spirit Woven. The happiness of her people was increased by her gentle sway. Their days of unbroken indolence rolled by without a single ripple to break upon the placid current. But this supreme happiness was about to close. The sad experiences that had already befallen some of the kindred nations, were about to afflict the people of the mild and lovely Zameaca.

At Isabella, on the north coast, the Spaniards having built a fortress and founded a city, we find the very reverse of the tranquillity that prevailed among the Ozamas. All the dignity of demeanor and rigid exaction of discipline from Columbus himself, assisted by the Adelantado, his brother Don Bartholemew, failed to entirely suppress the turbulence of those beneath them. A community made up of men of all classes of society at home, broken in fortune, incapable of, or rejecting, every moral restraint, adventurers, with no attachments among themselves, except such as enforced by the most harsh measures, it is natural to suppose, was in constant confusion. Personal encounters were common and frequent.

A young Arragonian, named Miguel Dias, in the service of the Adelantado, having engaged in a brawl with a comrade, and wounded him severely, in order to escape punishment, fled from the settlement attended by several others, who were either participants, or anxious to throw off the restraints of the Adelantado's strict government. Diaz and his companions wandered about in the forests, over mountains and plains, until they came in sight of the Ocean. They next came to an Indian village at the mouth of the river. The fugitives were travel-worn and exhausted. At first some surprise and alarm was manifested by the inhabitants, but this soon vanished, and the strangers were taken in and hospitably treated.

The young Arragonian, in all the parts of a man, was handsome and well formed, and his erect martial bearing was calculated to win applause. Diaz and his companions were the first the Ozamas had

4

seen of the strangers, and naturally they were objects of curiosity and almost veneration.

It was not long before in Zameaca's simple bosom a spark had found entrance that burst into a flame of love. The manly Arragonian, so far superior in attractions to her own subjects, had first won her admiration, she now found her whole being influenced by a more potent sway. Diaz observed this change. The rude nature of the soldier was not incapable of the softer passions of the lover. He was not insensible to the gentle influence stealing over him. He gave back his own heart's warm impulses for the tender tribute of the Queen. Bound in an union of reciprocal love, Diaz and his regal bride lived long and happily together.

Diaz, from a fugitive, now found himself the consort of a Queen. His companions mingled among the inhabitants, and history records no event to mar the residence of this handful of Spaniards among the mild-mannered natives upon the banks of the Ozama.

But this sunshine in the life of the Indian queen and her Castilian husband was not destined to pass on without some darkening shadows. A sense of isolation and uneasiness began to steal over the mind of Diaz. Thoughts of his countrymen and his native land once more broke upon him. He longed to return to the associations from which he felt himself debarred. The vigilant eye of love detected the altered manner of Diaz. The Queen observed his restlessness and seasons of moody contemplation. She was troubled at this change. With the unerring instinct of woman she at once divined the cause. With the natural diplomacy of her sex, she now thought only of providing against the calamity of losing the object of her deep-seated love. She resolved to entice the Spaniards to live within her dominions. How little did she know the fearful train of sorrows and misfortunes that would follow. But the strength of the Queen's attachment knew no limits—it knew no consequences other than the continuance of itself.

Zameaca knew that gold was the prize sought after by the stranger. She felt in this she held the talisman that would dissipate the chance of losing her husband. The Queen told Diaz of the abundance of gold not far off, and urged him to induce his countrymen to come and settle in the country. She even took him to the spot and pointed out the golden sands of the Hayna.

The effect was magical—Zameaca saw the change and rejoiced in the success of her fond hopes. Diaz felt that the tidings of his discovery would secure him toleration and pardon before the Adelantado. Taking his companions with him, and temporarily parting with his lovely and gentle Zameaca, Diaz set out for the seat of his countrymen, over fifty leagues distant, on the north side of the island. Still doubtful of the treatment they would receive, the returning fugitives entered the settlement clandestinely. Diaz now learned that his antagonist had recovered. Thus was the most serious cause of his anxiety removed. He at once boldly presented himself before the Adelantado asking forgiveness, at the same time revealing the rich discoveries he had made.

The time of the appearance of Diaz, and the welcome tidings he brought, were a great relief to the Adelantado. There was much dissatisfaction in Spain at the small returns which came in from the island. He now saw some chance of staying the discontent. Steps were at once set on foot to prove the veracity of the glowing accounts brought on by Diaz.

CHAPTER VII.

THE OCCUPATION OF THE HAYNA—FOUNDING OF SAN DOMINGO.

HE Adelantado was so much elated at this unexpected event, that he determined to visit, personally, the region so highly spoken of by Diaz. An armed force was organized, and, with the Adelantado, Miguel Diaz and Francisco de Garay at its head, started upon an expedition. The eager party hastened across the beautiful Vega to the fortress of Conception, and passing through a defile in a towering mountain range, struck into the charming plain of Bonao. The country through which they passed was generally high, and vegetation luxuriant. The Adelantado was constantly in raptures over the landscape and the extraordinary richness of the soil everywhere evident.

At last the explorers reached the Hayna, the

stream of which Diaz had told them. The Adelantado, imitated by all his followers, examined the sands in the stream, and found signs of an abundance of gold. Experiments were made and it was found that three drachms a day was a fair return. Everything had passed off to exceed his highest hopes. Diaz now found himself not only pardoned, but in high favor. He kept his faith with his Indian Queen. He hastened to her arms and comforted her inquietude by telling her of the satisfaction of his countrymen.

The Adelantado carried back to Isabella, where his brother the admiral was waiting, enthusiastic accounts of the result of his visit to the interior, and particularly of the boundless riches of the Hayna. To corroborate his statements, he produced some fine specimens of the wealth of the country. Columbus, delighted at this new light dawning upon his disappointment, ordered at once the building of a fortress on the Hayna and the working of the mines. Columbus as usual indulged in marvelous conjectures, and now believed, in his own mind, that he had at last struck the veritable treasures of Ophir. The existence of numerous excavations which resembled abandoned mines, gave force and credibility to these suppositions.

Columbus sailed for Spain and carried with him the tidings of new hopes to excite the cupidity and dazzle the morbid fancies of the government and the people of Spain.

In March, 1496, the Adelantado, leaving Don Diego Columbus at Isabella, again in person repaired, this time with a very large force of soldiers and workmen, to the Hayna and built a fort, which he called San Christoval. The brief presence of the Spaniards had already exerted an evil effect upon the natives. At first hospitable, they were now morose and distant. It was impossible to subsist so large a force without the co-operation of the people of the country, their refusal to grant supplies now necessitated the sending of the larger part of the troops to enjoy the abundance of the Vega.

In the summer of the same year the arrival of three caravals, with reinforcements, at Isabella, also brought letters from Columbus directing the building of a town and seaport at the mouth of the Ozama. The Adelantado repaired to the spot, and found Zameaca and the possessor of her unfortunate love living happily together. The eastern bank of the river was chosen as the site of the future city. A fortress was built, called New Isabella. A garrison of twenty men was left to hold it. Soon after, the city was transferred to the west bank, where it now stands, and at the same time received its present name. Zameaca clung to the object of her devotion with all that passionate tenderness of which only a true and lovely woman is capable. The union was blessed with two children; and Zameaca, to further surrender her very being, abandoned the religion of her ancestors. She was baptized in the Christian faith, and, as if to obliterate all traces of her birth and race, took the name of Catalina.

But a sorrowful change had taken place in the strangers whom the queen had invited to her dominions. From recipients of hospitality, they now became arrogant and overbearing. Her association with Miguel Diaz, though it gave her a few moments of earthly joy, had ruined the happiness of a whole people. The severest acts of tyranny and barbarity were practised. The queen had lent, at first, the services of her subjects to assist the strangers in erecting suitable structures for their comfort and accommodation. These services were soon found to be indispensable, and when the queen claimed her people back, the strangers refused to yield them, and rivetted upon them the chains of lasting slavery.

Diaz was made the first Alcalde of the new-born city, and afterwards held several offices of trust and responsibility with credit to himself and fidelity to the authorities over him.

The lovely Zameaca, none the less devoted to her husband, brooded over the calamities that had befallen her people. No longer able to sustain herself under the trying circumstances of their sufferings, and an inward gnawing of self-accusation that all had resulted from her own acts, Zameaca suddenly left her home, her children, and her people, and was never after seen. No trace of the manner nor place of her death, nor even the slightest hint of the whereabouts of her body, ever came to light to clear the mystery of the sad end of the unhappy Zameaca.

The events which followed the untimely fate of the Queen and the bondage of her subjects, were the occupation of the entire southern country, and the completion, in the very midst of the hitherto peaceful and contented homes of the Ozamas, of a city which was to be the capital of the island, the seat of domestic trade, and the emporium of commerce.

The discovery of the mines of the Hayna had given a fresh impetus to the flocking to the island of a large number of adventurers and vagabonds, the most despicable, worthless, blood-thirsty, and fiendish set that ever afflicted any land.

The unhealthy atmosphere in the vicinity of Isabella, as well as the comparative sterility of the surrounding country, had long excited a desire in the mind of Columbus to make a change. The pure air and fertility of the southern coast answered all the requirements of a permanent city. In view of these facts, Isabella was no longer to be the seat of empire and authority on the island. The place was abandoned and allowed to go to decay, while at the mouth of the Ozama sprung up a rival city, destined to become the centre of the most eventful occurrences and the starting point of the most thrilling maritime adventures that the world had ever seen. The wealth of the island poured in, and regardless of iniquitous administration, and constant disorder inflicted by arrogant governors, and embittered factions, San Domingo grew in population and importance. It was from the island came the means for fitting out most of the expeditions that gave to the Castilian crown the golden lands of Mexico and Peru, besides other vast territories in the tropics and on the southern continent of America. It was at the city that these expeditions, generally, were fitted out, or manned, came to prepare for renewing their hazardous voyages, or returned to rest after braving unparalleled dangers, and meeting more frequently with bitter disappointment. It was from here that

that zealous and invincible spirit Alonzo de Ojeda, the discoverer of Venezuela, carried on his career of marvelous exploration and escape; and it was here, also, that he died and was buried.

Francisco Pizarro, the conqueror of Peru, embarked from the city with Ojeda on the hazardous expedition to Darien, which led to the subsequent events of the romantic life of this stern and inflexible explorer. Fernando Cortez, the conqueror of the vast empire of the Montezumas, was here in 1504. The bachelor, Fernandez de Encisco, more plethoric in purse than in brains, set out from here in search of Ojeda, in his ill-fated expedition to Darien. Vasco Nuñez de Balboa was the companion of the bachelor, Encisco. While the master was scouring the ocean, in search of the vessels and means that he had placed at the disposal of the reckless Ojeda, Balboa penetrated the interior, and the first of his race, planted his vision upon the tranquil blue waters of the Pacific.

Indeed San Domingo was a sort of hive, from which, in that age of daring, nearly all the explorations, which excite the admiration and astonishment of living generations, were sent out.

In her palmiest days her name was associated with some of the greatest events of history. Her principal citizens all took their part in the drama of the period. Her affluence was enormous. In addition to enterprise at sea, the ruins of her numerous churches and convents testify that her citizens did not neglect to contribute a liberal share of their possessions to the development and extension of the Kingdom of God.

Where three centuries ago wealth and luxury reigned the traveler now finds poverty and decay. Such is the instability of human affairs. Such the perishable and changing nature of the most enduring works of the hand of man.

CHAPTER VIII.

A VISIT TO THE PRESIDENT OF THE REPUBLIC—THE CABINET.

AT the earliest moment after my arrival on the island, I made known my wish to pay my respects to the President. Through the courtesy of Señor Curiel, Minister of the Treasury, this wish was communicated and favorably responded to. Owing, however, to the severe indisposition of the President, several days had passed before my purpose was carried out. The regular presidential "palace" was pointed out on our way, facing the Plaza. Instead, however, of taking possession of this spacious residence, the President lived in a very unpretending dwelling. The building, as he afterwards told me, was his own property. The country, he said, was entirely too much embarrassed and impoverished, to sustain the extravagance of a more expensive establishment.

Passing from the Plaza, along a narrow street, under the shadow of the time-worn walls of the Cathedral, we turned to the right, into another street. We had proceeded but a short distance further, when we reached the end of our walk. A small detachment of native soldiers, the President's body-guard, were lounging about in front of the building, while two sentinels were posted on duty on either side of the entrance. We were courteously met by the officer of the guard and were shown in through a wide arched and paved passage, to a broad stair-case leading up to a spacious balcony in the rear. Another officer and sentinels were stationed here, and also several couriers or orderlies were in waiting.

Having deposited our umbrellas and hats, we were politely bowed into a large apartment used as an audience chamber. Here we were received by Minister Del Monte, who presented us to his colleagues, Hungria and Gautier. Minister Curiel, who was also present, I had met before, and therefore we exchanged civilities without the preliminary of an introduction.

While the American consul, who accompanied me, was making a few preliminary general remarks, I took occasion to gratify a little inclination to gaze about. Everything around was in the utmost simplicity. The ceiling and walls were perfectly plain, and white-washed. Several maps were hanging about the room. The floor was of red bricks. The furniture consisted of a very antique specimen of a sofa, and a few chairs. In one corner was a desk, covered with papers, used by Minister Gautier. Outside, on the balcony, were several benches and a hat-rack.

The ministers, from the beginning, struck me as very superior men. Their conversations upon general topics, the affairs of the world at large, or the domestic concerns of their own beautiful island, were equally free, well-considered, discreet, and satisfactory. I was not able, in so brief a space as an interview of an hour, to make any distinctions in regard to any of the gentlemen I met, in point of ability to fill their important and responsible spheres.

Manuel Maria Gautier, whose office corresponded to our Secretary of State, impressed me as a man of diplomatic skill. He had the first elements, at least reticence; a refined, affable, and still reserved manner; or, when necessary, a supply of well-rounded compliments. He was a middle-aged man, small in stature, with a Spanish face, white complexion, and a strikingly keen and passionate eye. After we had seated ourselves, he returned to his desk and kept up a vigorous writing, stopping occasionally to put in a word or two, or to ask a question.

General José Hungria, the Minister of War and Navy, was a tall, fine-looking gentleman, of very dark complexion. His manners were pleasant, and he displayed quite a disposition to converse. He was about fifty years of age, and, I was informed, wielded great influence in the northern part of the island. It was he, I was told, who led the movement which resulted in the overthrow of Cabral and the reinstatement of Baez in the presidency. I judged that the General, in addition to possessing fine abilities, had a cautious mind, a rare capacity for command, and invincible purpose.

Ricardo Curiel, Secretary of the Treasury, was small in figure, dark brunette in complexion, and, apparently, less than forty years of age. He was of an emphatically nervous temperament—quick, witty, and talkative, with an unusual amount of vivacity in his actions and conversation, and activity in his public duty. The fiscal condition of the island being at a very low ebb, the responsibility upon the hands of Señor Curiel was not great. His best strokes of financial policy consisted in how to keep all the parts of the government together and in motion, without money. His plans seemed to work well, for, at the time of my visit, the treasury was reported without a dollar, and no prospects of very speedily getting in a supply of that necessary aliment of sound government.

Felix Delmonte, the Minister of Justice and Public Instruction, was, physically, a spare man, with a face tending to the Jewish caste. He appeared to be the oldest of the ministers, and still was not over fifty. He had liberal views, and, unquestionably, added intelligence to the administration. It was afterwards mentioned to me that he was not an uninfluenced appointment, but that he had been in "asylum"— that is, had taken refuge in a consulate, (in this case, that of the United States,) to escape the ire of the new authorities that had come into power—and was, after pointing out the false impressions of the government, put into the official position which he held when I met him. He was evidently of a social turn, and did more than all the rest to entertain us.

We had waited about ten minutes, the time passing pleasantly in conversation with the ministers, when President Baez entered from an adjoining room. He warmly greeted Consul Smith, after which I was introduced by the Minister of Justice. Asking us again to be seated the President himself occupied a rocking chair close by. I was very favorably impressed at once. In appearance, manner, and conversation, he appeared like a man of true principles and extraordinary ability. He was a master of the French language, having received a portion of his education in Paris. In his style of conversation he was ready, but it had a subdued tone, and all his remarks were well weighed, as if he felt the importance of giving no cue to be used against him by his enemies. Physically, he was about the average height, of good figure, and full flesh. He had a brunette face, slightly "off color," intelligent, and of very agreeable expression. His eyes were black, and wore an appearance of fire, indicating strong feeling, and nervous activity. He displayed an extensive production in the shape of side whiskers. The only striking evidence of negro blood coursing in his veins was detected by his wool, instead of hair. Baez was about sixty years of age, though he looked much younger.

CHAPTER IX.

AN INTERVIEW.

WAS much gratified at the readiness with which the President conversed. Observing this, I did not hesitate to bring up questions of more interest than mere common-place civilities. I took down, after my return to the consulate, an abstract of the conversation, which I give below.

I had remarked that it was a great misfortune that a country, so rich in natural productions, should be so harrassed and impoverished by constant uprisings against the government.

The President replied: "I am glad to hear you express that fact." I see that you realize our situation, and I hope when you return to your own Great Republic in the north you will mention your impressions to those of your government that you may meet. All of us, who have the welfare of our poor country at heart, appreciate this unfortunate state of affairs, and deprecate the necessity of spending nearly all our small means in keeping down a few bad men, men who keep the country constantly in confusion and alarm. If this were a popular movement we would all consider it time to give up the authority to other hands, but it is not so. The people in the rural districts are for peace, quiet, and secure government, so that they can work their few acres, and not be disturbed by constant anxiety. The business men are also for order, because it is very plain that mercantile and commercial activity cannot thrive where there is uncertainty. Yet all this unhappy state of affairs, suspension of industry, and stagnation of business, results from a handful of fugitives from justice, and desperadoes, who have established themselves on the Haytien border, for no other purpose than to plunder. Of course, if they can succeed in doing so, they will depose all of us, and place themselves in authority.

"I have been in public life many years. I was a member of the Constitutional Assembly of '44, and took a prominent part in framing the constitutional convention promulgated at that time. I made a speech, and had carried that clause of the constitution which accords equal rights to all men.

I have several times been elevated to the Presidency of the Republic. That is a position of no profit, so that I was certainly not inwardly urged to it by mercenary motives. As for the power it placed in my hands, I was responsible for the exercise of that power, and have always striven to use it mildly, and for the good of the people worthy of its lenient exercise.

"We have some desperate diseases, and are very often obliged to apply desperate remedies, but it has always been my course, when in places of power, to use desperate remedies only where there are hopeless cases."

I replied, in order to change the subject, that, as far as I could learn, I thought his government was very wise, and I had yet to hear the first word against it. I mentioned that I intended visiting the interior of the island.

The President replied: "Am very glad to hear that, and before you leave I will hand you letters of introduction to the governors of the districts you intend to visit. These may be of assistance to you in the way of comfort and information. You say you will travel from Puerto Plata to the capital. That will lead you through some of our finest country. You will see that nature has done much for us;

but we are going backward, instead of forward, and it is hard to tell what is to become of us and all our natural resources. First, the outrageous and unrelenting devastation, incident to the evacuation of the island by the Spaniards, the invasions from Hayti, the French, and the English, and the necessity of the Dominican people to turn their attention to war instead of agriculture, have been the causes that have brought us down to our present situation. As I say, you will see an unparalleled country, but desolation and ruin everywhere. It will not be like traveling in your own prosperous and peaceable country. It will be like traveling through a wilderness, with all the inconveniences of no roads, no bridges, and no places of rest by the way at night. You will have a severe journey. This being the rainy season, you must expect to get drenched, you must expect mud, you must expect to swim swollen rivers, you must expect to swing your hammock and make your camp-fire in the dark forest. Think of a traveler like yourself, with the means to be comfortable, compelled to submit to such hardships in such a country. It cuts me to the soul to think of it, but I am powerless. You will see abandoned estates, and other evidences of former wealth, and prosperity. You will then be able to judge what San Domingo was in the days of prosperity, and what she is in her time of trial and misfortune."

I remarked that indeed it was a melancholy spectacle, but had he no hope?

The President continued: "Certainly I have hope, we all have hope, but what good will that do us unless we can take hold of something stronger than ourselves, and be supported. It would not be long before we could help ourselves. We are now getting lower and lower every year. If this state of things goes on, we are hopelessly gone."

Here I put in a word, asking what were his wishes?

The President replied: "We look to your government. If we had your strong arm to lift us up, you would see how soon we would be able to return all your assistance."

THE AUTHOR: What kind of help do you want?

THE PRESIDENT: Well, we would have to receive more than moral support. We are now in penury, absolute penury. You are the only people that we would have anything to do with. Your government is a republic; that is the spirit of the American continent. We have had Spanish dominion, we have had French rule, and we have had English interference, and invariably the fidelity of the people to their institutions has been successful in driving back these invasions of the country and usurpation of the government. We would require tangible support in the way of money, and in return we might give a lease of the great Bay of Samana, with the adjacent peninsula.

THE AUTHOR: Would you not part with the bay and peninsula?

THE PRESIDENT: If necessary we might, but there is a feeling of pride in the breast of the people against the alienation of territory.

THE AUTHOR: Then go in for annexation by asking for it. Here is a valuable island, of great natural wealth, useless to you because of your misfortunes, and for the same reasons useless to the world. I have no doubt the United States would favorably consider your overtures of annexation. You would then have a firm government at once. You will pardon the liberty of this suggestion.

THE PRESIDENT: The suggestion needs no pardon, as we have oftened considered the same subject ourselves, and we agree that all would be benefited; but such a movement would have its enemies, and although a great majority would be in favor, we have no strength to court a controversy with the minority. We are powerless to act independently, as we could not face the opposition. All these things take means, which we have not.

THE AUTHOR: Then how do you propose to inaugurate the scheme? The United States certainly could not lead off in the matter.

THE PRESIDENT: No, I understand that; but what we need is the assurance of coöperation, so that when we move there will be no disappointment to leave us in the lurch. In the case of the Samana negotiations, a few years ago, with Mr. Seward, we were left in an awkward predicament. It was thought everything was accommodated to the result, but Mr. Seward's course compelled us to withdraw, when on the very eve of success. In a great movement like that, it is as depressing to its friends if it fails, as it imbitters enemies if it wins. That was a lesson, and we cannot afford to ignore the experience.

THE AUTHOR: There should be no trouble now about consummating a sale of the bay and peninsula to the United States, I think. I would hardly know what to say about leasing. I do not think it would be our policy. But at all events there is a Chief Magistrate, at the head of the nation now, who will stand by his promises. He has a sense of responsibility and obligation in affairs of state as much as he has in his own private affairs. This is not always the case in international transactions. This you know by experience.

THE PRESIDENT: What do you think would be the best course to pursue?

THE AUTHOR: If you wish to dispose of the bay, or even annex the island, and transfer the jurisdiction to the United States, say so, and begin your advances at once. This will be confidential, and should you fail to get a response from the United States, the enemies of such a stroke of state policy would be none the wiser.

THE PRESIDENT: I have always done the best I could to advance the interests of my country and my fellow-citizens. I do not think there is any person who can stand up and accuse me in that. There are many who oppose me, and denounce my course. They call me a tyrant and everything else, but that does not make it so. These gentleman, (pointing to his ministers,) know how I am situated. They know the exigencies of the island. I candidly think that we have but one sure course to pursue, and I plainly mention it, and in this my ministers agree with me, that course is annexation. (The ministers all expressed accordance.) So the country once more lifts her head and prospers, I feel no hesitation under the circumstances, in taking any steps. I think an act consummated from honest motives, will, at least, receive the applause of all right thinking men of the world. I repeat what I have said, if the United States Government be willing to accept the jurisdiction of the island, I am ready at once to hand over my share in its rule, and will, after, devote my life to the service of aiding all in my power, the course of progress and prosperity which will then open before my country.

I was heartily surprised, and certainly much gratified, to hear such sound statesmanship from a man belonging to a race that has labored against so many disadvantages. As our stay had already been rather long, I made one of those quietly suggestive starts, which was taken by the consul, as a hint to leave. After observing the usual forms of a courteous separation, we both apologized for detaining the President so much from the affairs of state. Having, in return, received a request to call again, when we could resume our conversation, we left the executive presence for the consulate.

I was entirely satisfied, in my own mind, of the patriotism of Baez and all those associated with him. I was equally assured that they sorely lamented the distraction which constantly prevailed, and impoverished the island. I was certainly convinced that there were no other than the most exalted motives for the expressed desire to join the destiny of the island with that of the United States.

The day after our visit, a dinner was given on board the Tybee, in response to the courtesies of the Government. The President and Ministers were present. Toasts and speeches were exchanged, and the party separated with the best of feeling.

CHAPTER X.

EXCURSION TO THE CAVES OF SANTA ANNA.

FIVE miles from the capital are the caves of Santa Anna, so called, it is said, after an individual of occult powers, who exorcised the indigenous spirits of the island, which resorted there.

As these caves were interesting, both from their singular character, physically, and equally so in the associations which gathered about them, I took the first opportunity to visit them. My companions were several of the passengers from the steamer.

We had secured two decrepit specimens of the animal kingdom, resembling horses, as a sort of relief on the journey. It was found that this was the best we could do, unless the rest would consent to occupy a rickety vehicle, evidently designed and manufactured some time during the Spanish era. Those who were not accommodated with something to place between themselves and the earth, after considering every thing, preferred to make the journey on foot.

One beautiful morning, such as is seldom found elsewhere in the tropics, we set out from the steamer, and riding by the main street across the city, left by the gate La Separation (*Condé*) in the western wall. Passing a cemetery by the road-side we entered, at a short distance, a scene of the wildest profusion of beauty, of color, and of exquisite vegetable forms. Our way lay by a narrow path, on either side lined with every variety of tropical plants, from the gigantic mahogany tree down to the most diminutive and delicate blade of grass. Overhead was a drapery of green branches and fragrant flowers, often completely closing out the rays of the sun.

The scene was unexampled. It equalled, if it did not surpass in variety and beauty of Flora, the most famous islands of the Asiatic tropics. It was one constant bewildering enchantment. The senses were completely overpowered. Everything had returned to its primitive wildness, and but for our own consciousness of the capital of a State so near by, it might have been thought that we had entered a region which the invading hand of man had never penetrated.

After a delightful experience of two hours, we

reached a sudden rise in the surface. Passing around a small cluster of undergrowth we stood by an abrupt wall of earth and rock. In front was an opening sufficient for us to pass through, leading the horses. This natural archway was about six feet high and twelve feet in width. Within we entered a perfect amphitheatre, nearly a hundred yards in diameter, and overgrown with trees and plants of the most beautiful varieties. As a physical wonder, that before us was more remarkable and peculiar, than extensive in its proportions. A circular space had apparently become detached from the contiguous surface, and by some convulsion of nature had sunk about thirty feet. The surrounding walls thus formed consisted of a corallaceous rock. It was evident, from the visible traces of the action of water, that the formation had at some period been submerged.

From the upper rim of the wall grew a variety of wild vines, which hung over like drapery. In the rocky portions were numerous caverns, large and small, some connected with each other by intricate windings, extending far into the dark bowels of the earth.

Our party undertoook the exploration of this subterranean labyrinth. We were encountered at the entrance by innumerable bats, which took on such unpleasant familiarities, during their random flights, as to suddenly arrest their momentum in our faces, to seek shelter in our hair, and particularly did they exercise a wonderful facility of extinguishing our candles. One of the caves we entered through a narrow hole in the rock. One of our number, possessing more than the average breadth of beam, here found difficulty in penetrating, but, after considerable effort, forced his way through. After creeping along a narrow passage we came into a small chamber. The minute crystals which had formed on the rocky walls sparkled in the light of our candles with dazzling effect. We pushed on over a confusion of rocks and other impediments, creeping through the smallest apertures. We saw a number of tributary passages, leading off in both directions. We, however, kept on the straight course, until finally, after a toilsome journey, we came suddenly into day-light. We now found ourselves in the open country, outside the circular space from which we had entered, and quite a distance off.

We returned to the caves and indulged in a lunch we had brought with us.

During the lifetime of Zameaca her subjects were, in a measure, protected through the influence of the reciprocal attachment existing between the Queen and her husband. But still the pangs of remorse sank deep into her very soul when she contemplated the unhappiness that had befallen her people. She reproached herself for the innocent and unthinking union that had caused so much woe.

After the disappearance of Zameaca, the fiendish brutality of the Spaniards let loose upon the now entirely unprotected subjects of the departed Queen. During her life, she had loaned her people to assist the Spaniards in building their city. Having thus had a taste of the benefits of their labor, and the interposition of the Queen being no longer in existence to stay their infamous purposes, the survivors were reduced to hopeless slavery. Their sad lot becoming unendurable they fled from the oppression of the Spaniards, and took refuge in the numerous caves near the scene of their misery. Here they vainly hoped to escape a cruel bondage.

It was in the caves of Santa Anna that three hundred Ozamas secreted themselves. It was here, in former days, that Zameaca's happy people retired from their sacred palm groves to worship, through the Zemis—the messengers or intercessors—their one Supreme Being, who inhabited the sky. It was here the Butios, or Priests, painted and tatooed, fasted and performed ablutions. It was here, after throwing themselves into a phrensy of physical piety and mental aberration by drinking a decoction made out of a powder from certain herbs, they pretended to transmit from the Zemis to their credulous followers the mandates of their God.

Here, also, the people. on occasions proclaimed by the Cacique, gathered for high festival in honor of the intercessory gods. The married adorned themselves in the best of their primitive attire; the unmarried came naked. The Cacique seated himself. His subjects entered with tribute. When these had been laid before the gods, the females sang and danced, and recounted the deeds of the Caciques of early days. Where a happy and contented people once went to worship as they had been taught by their ancestors, those who had not already passed away, a sacrifice to the severity of their task-masters, now sought escape from hopeless and savage bondage. To these caves came the remaining Caciques and influential men of the tribe. They were fed by the people, and for a brief space prolonged their existence unharrassed by their relentless oppressors. But their masters pursued them, and, having smoked them from their subterranean places of refuge, they were put to death, without the slightest form of accusation, or any other offence than an attempt to avoid an existence infinitely worse than death.

The numerous caverns on the island played an important part in all the religious ceremonies and belief of the primitive people. In their idea of the creation, the natives believed that man first made his appearance in the world from a cavern. One time, while walking in the forest, he spied a strange animal, which he caught but could not hold. Other men, aflicted with a sort of disease which gave rough hands, at length seized and held captive four. The animals were found to be women, and from these the world was peopled.

CHAPTER XI.

CELEBRATION OF THE FESTIVAL OF CORPUS CHRISTI—
A THEATRICAL PERFORMANCE.

WHILE still waiting for the steamer to complete her cargo, I had an opportunity of witnessing the festival of Corpus Christi. A party was made up and attended the spacious and ancient church of San Domingo, where the ceremonies were to take place. The city throughout was liberally decorated with the bunting of all nations. In fact, anything that had the appearance of a flag was thrown from the windows and roofs of the houses. The rich displayed the Dominican colors kept for this and similar days of religious or political jubilee. The resident Roman Catholic subjects of other nations also displayed their own national ensigns. The poor contented themselves with strips of muslin or flannel, or sometimes manifested their pious ardor in a red flannel petticoat or a white shirt picturesquely waving in the breeze.

On the open space, in front of the church, a great number of citizens, with their wives and families, had gathered to witness the procession bearing the host. A detachment of troops, consisting of sixty bare-footed, bare-backed men and boys, armed with rusty, flint-lock muskets, was drawn up, with the garrison band, in front of the main entrance.

We walked inside the building and took a position near one of the side chapels, or alcoves, from which a fine view of the entire church could be had. The great altar, with its massive front of silver and antique carving, was decorated with flowers and lighted with great numbers of candles. Upon the brick floors were hundreds of kneeling worshipers. As we entered, the organ was boldly rendering its accompaniments while the choir performed the appropriate services of the day. Then, in turn, the solemn intonations of the priest broke in upon the volume of harmony, and gave that peculiar variation of sound which always impresses the mind with a sense of solemnity. In the midst of these forms the great bell tolled, and in response to its solemn waves of sound every head bent in prayer, while the priest held aloft the monstrance containing the Sacred Wafer.

After the preliminary ceremonies had concluded, the priests, cross-bearers, acolytes, and boys, in all their paraphernalia, formed in the centre of the church. A priest, arrayed in costly and glittering surplice, stood under a canopy of silk borne by four attendant priests, and before him held the monstrance. In front, also, stood a priest, with rosary and ritual; while behind, other priests and choiresters, altar-boys and worshipers, bearing lighted tapers, formed.

At a given signal, the great tones of the organ burst forth in appropriate symphony. The bell in the tower again tolled. The solemn procession moved forward and filed out of the church. The moment the Host appeared, the crowd and soldiers in the open air removed their hats, fell upon their knees, and remained in that attitude until the priests, with their charge, had passed.

The crowd now rose to their feet. The troops, led by the band, formed in the procession. The players struck up a medley of sounds not very solemnly inspiring, but might have answered at a Hindoo exorcising of the spirit of the devil. Lacking this disturbing element, the scene was extremely impressive.

The procession moved through the principal streets.

As it passed along, the people came out of their houses and knelt down in solemn homage. The procession then returned to the church, and the pious duties of the day were over.

The same evening, in company with Señor Curiel, I attended the theatre. The Sabbath was the gala-day of the citizens of San Domingo. The theatrical company was a family concern, composed of a father and mother, and several daughters and sons, who did the heavy business, and were assisted by two walking gentlemen from Havana. The rest of the players were made up of native aspirants for histrionic fame. The performances were given but once a week, in an ancient and spacious building, which, in the days of glory and prosperity on the island, was used as a college. We elbowed our way through a noisy crowd congregated in front. In the main entrance the man at the ticket window was loudly indulging in a verbal altercation with some recreant patron of the establishment. We were escorted up a wide pair of stairs, into a sort of balcony, from which the audience, as well as the play, could be seen to advantage. The interior was lighted with candles or kerosene lamps, which cast a dingy light upon the few hundred dusky spectators. The actors and actresses, producing their respective dramatic effects in the feeble rays of a few flickering and sickly foot-lights, looked like so many spectres. One moment in a phrensy of madness, they strode backwards and forwards across the stage, as if they were about to let loose an avalanche of passion—again, they soothed down into mollified anger, or irreconcilable despair.

A liberal supply of bunting relieved the bare and dilapidated walls. The interior fittings were extremely primitive, consisting of pine benches. By way of extra accommodations, for those who possessed more means, and, naturally, sensitive sitting attributes, a few chairs were provided. Around the great hall there were a number of balconies and alcoves, which were occupied by the better class of citizens, with their wives and daughters. Below were the common people.

It was a few minutes after nine o'clock in the evening when we joined the patient and martyr audience. The performance had been going on for an hour. The chief affliction of the evening was "*El mal de Ojo,*" the Evil-eye. An enraged monster of a biped was addressing in a most irate manner, both physically and vocally, a diminutive and passive female, who rejoined in a sickly tone. At times, by way of stage effect, the female threw her head in sundry attitudes, and judiciously rolled a pair of orbs overflowing with grief and womanly submission. The latter optical demonstrations were not minutely discernable from my point of observation, owing particularly to a deficiency in the powers of the faint luminaries, scuffling here and there, at great odds, against outright darkness.

This scene having lasted through a painful duration, our angered friend retired behind the scenes, some one having come to his relief. This individual was also out of temper, but instead of lecturing in a single attitude, he went tearing up and down the stage, with sufficient velocity and vehemence to have very soon exhausted a person of less wind. After this performance had been repeated several times, with all due recognition of the courtesy of the occasion, and a deep sense of repentance, I made some inquiries in regard to the termination of the play. When informed, sometime between two or three o'clock in the morning, the precise hour being uncertain, it struck me that the people would get their money's worth. I certainly would have taken a very small bid for my interest.

I wore my patience through till midnight, having caught several naps in an off-hand way, greatly to the resuscitation of my energies. But the climax of my despair was reached, so as gracefully as I could, under the circumstances, I called in the assistance of several time-honored and unquestionable excuses. I now left the players and their heroic spectators to their mutual indulgence.

CHAPTER XII.

OFF FOR SAMANA—THE DOMINICAN FLEET IN TOW—
A NAVAL ENGAGEMENT.

IT was now one week since the arrival of the Tybee. Having received her cargo, she was ready to resume her voyage to Samana bay. The government had received intelligence of the presence of a steamer hostile to the Dominican flag, commanded by Gregorio Luperon, a refugee, and an officially proclaimed outlaw. This state of belligerence existing at Samana was a damper upon our voyage, and particularly upon my own contemplated peregrinations on the peninsula. It was still proposed to visit that section and reconnoitre. We took on board forty soldiers to reinforce the patriotic inhabitants of Santa Barbara and the peninsula. General José Hungria, the Minister of War and Marine, was also a passenger.

It was eight o'clock in the morning. As our

steamer ploughed out of the quiet current of the Ozama, a large crowd of citizens assembled at the wharf and upon the walls of the city overlooking the river. The band also performed several strange and novel airs. Cheers and waving of handkerchiefs were exchanged.

Outside of the bar, we took in tow the Alta Gracia, an eighty-ton, armed schooner, destined for Samana. The next afternoon we overhauled the sister schooner, Capotilla, and also took her in tow, she making fast astern the Alta Gracia. We now cut a formidable figure. Our old ship led the way; next came about ten or twelve fathoms of cable; next, the Alta Gracia; next, the same length of cable; and in the rear, the Capotilla. We had thus hanging to us the entire navy of the Republic—a scene not often witnessed—the maritime power of an independent state strung on twenty or thirty fathoms of cable.

Our steamer kept on her way, but with a material diminution of speed, and with incessant delays caused by the parting of the cables. It was not until noon of the third day after leaving the Ozama, that we hove in sight of the head-lands at the entrance to the bay. A dense mist prevailed, which enabled the steamer to tow the schooners to the windward of the main channel without discovery. Under cover of a bold and precipitous promontory, the detachment of Dominican soldiers on board were transferred from the steamer. Every preparation having been made for immediate action, the steamer headed for the bay. By this time the rain which fell in the morning had subsided, and the mist, dispelled by the intense heat of the sun, had entirely disappeared. The shores, through the bright atmosphere, looked beautifully fresh and green. Having rounded an isolated and solitary peak, known to modern mariners as "Sloop Rock," the whole beautiful, broad, majestic expanse of the bay burst into view. We were now fairly within the head-lands. Eight miles distant, anchored by a small island rising out of the quiet bosom of the bay, was the hostile steamer. She was painted black, and presented a sharp, narrow, head-view. She stood high out of the water, and carried two funnels. Near by was a large steamer with one funnel, and flying the American colors. I afterwards learned this was the Hero, of New York, on her way to ply on one of the South American rivers. She had run into the bay for fuel, and had been detained by the pirate. There was also a small captured schooner anchored by the vessel. It must have been with some sensations of surprise and consternation that Luperon discovered us steaming directly for him. With the assistance of glasses, it was not difficult to perceive that the decorum of the pirate crew was considerably disturbed. A few moments before, Luperon and his men were lolling about on deck, taking advantage of every wave of the sultry air. They were now hastening to all parts of the vessel, getting the guns ready for action and raising steam. From the accounts I afterwards received, the steamer had run in out of coal, and intended laying in a supply from the veins on the peninsula. The people, however, had rallied and drove off the crew. They next prevented them from landing, which compelled them to take on a supply of wood from a different part of the coast.

Gregorio Luperon, who was in command of the Telegrafo, (Telegraph,) had some time before been banished, on account of his turbulent spirit and persistent efforts to overthrow the existing government. He repaired to the island of St. Thomas. Here, with the assistance of partizans and a few friends, he managed to secure a steamer, in which, with a crew of the hard cases of all nations, he set out on a piratical cruise along the Dominican coast. The worst feature in the affair was the fact that the vessel was enabled, through the connivance of a few Americans, to leave the harbor of St. Thomas under the American flag, after she had been refused clearance under other colors.

After alarming the whole coast, and, under the Venezuelan flag, having fired upon the town of Puerto Plata, with a few small craft she had captured, she ran into Samana Bay.*

It was evident that we were involved in the fight, having towed the two schooners around from the capital. With this strong argument in his mind, and but one rusty cannon to support any belligerent ideas that he might have felt at any time during these preliminary scenes, our captain determined to to give the pirate plenty of room.

The steamer had now towed the schooners within less than three miles of the objective craft. Orders were given "to let go" and in a few minutes more, Leon Glas, High Admiral of the fleets of the Dominican Republic, with the entire naval force of his government, spread his sails and steered bravely for the pirate.

---

* The same night, immediately on the heels of our departure, the pirate left the bay, and steamed to the island of Tortola, where she was seized, and her crew disbanded. The United States Steamer Seminole, as soon as the news reached the head-quarters of the Navy, was sent in pursuit, but it does not appear that anything was done in the matter.

The schooners, depending solely upon the fickle wind for their motive power, labored under every disadvantage, and certainly displayed unusual daring in the manner in which they steered their course directly on the pirate. From the other side there were signs of life. In a remarkably short time the pirate got up steam, and before the Dominicans got within fair cannon-shot, the escape of the vaporous power indicated that Luperon was not as impotent as had been supposed.

After the schooners had set out on their perilous mission, our steamer stopped engines and drifted about in sight, in order to catch a glimpse at the fight, and to learn the result. There was an expectation on the part of the Dominicans, that the schooner would succeed in reaching the Telegrafo before she got up steam, in which case it was the intention to board. Such a chance of good fortune was soon dispelled, for it was seen that steam was up, and it became necessary to adopt a new style of naval manœuvre. Each schooner carried an old fashioned eighteen pounder brass gun, mounted "midships," on a pivot. The courageous little fleet left us under full sail, advancing on the starboard tack, until within fair range. The Telegrafo fired the first gun, the shot flying high. She now displayed two guns, which were fired in rapid succession. The little fleet kept on their course, but observing the enemy preparing to set out to meet them, took a position almost broadside, at about a thousand yards, and between the hostile steamer and the town of Santa Barbara.

It was not until after her eighth shot that the Dominicans replied from the Capotilla. The first shot put a ball into the prominent hull of the Telegrafo. The engagement now became quite brisk. Puffs of white smoke, and after a few seconds the interchanging reverberations of the conflict, could be seen and heard from our steamer. To us the contest was exceedingly exciting, the diminutive fleet carrying with it our most earnest hopes of victory, was closely watched with our glasses. The practice from both the schooners was astonishingly accurate The Capotilla, during the earlier stage of the action, received one shot about a foot above her boom, putting a good sized rent in her sail. The pirate having at last raised sufficient steam to venture on the offensive, weighed anchor and started in pursuit of the schooners. But the little fleet was prudently and well handled. Having taken up an advantageous position in the beginning as soon as it was seen that the Telegrafo was in motion, the schooners headed for the land under cover of the guns of Santa Barbara. It was a tight race. Certainly at one time, for my part, I had lost all hope for the safety of the vessels. The Telegrafo having the advantage of steam, could take her own course and was bearing down upon the schooners when she was received with a brisk fusilade from the soldiers on board. Having no bow-chaser, the steamer was unable to return the fire of the Dominicans.

The schooners having made the protecting harbor of Santa Barbara, in unison with the shore batteries gave a lively reception, insomuch that the Telegrafo hauled off and took up a new position. The combatants now engaged in an animated consumption of powder and exchange of iron. From appearances the Telegrafo was getting the worst of the entertainment, for after firing a few guns with great rapidity she suddenly ceased and moved, by steaming very slowly and apparently in a crippled condition, back to her old anchorage. As she moved out of range the brave little fleet sent a parting shot, which could be followed ricochetting across the water in close proximity to the discomfited craft of Gregorio Luperon.

The action fairly began about half past four o'clock in the afternoon and lasted until nearly sunset,

While the engagement was going on a boat's crew communicated with us from the American steamer. The captain sent to ask coals, which we could not furnish, whereupon the crew returned. We learned from this source that the Telegrafo had on board thirty prisoners taken from the shore, who were used to chop wood.

There was no doubt in any one's mind that could Luperon reach us we would not be most courteously treated. A council of war was held. It was determined to lay in the outer bay all night under steam, in hopes of being able to get in the next day. To be prepared for emergencies all the stores belonging to the Dominican soldiers were landed on the beach in canoes, also a quantity of powder and shell. General Hungria at the same time went ashore, proposing to go by land to the town and assume command. Hardly had these arrangements been completed than the Telegrafo was discovered in the dim light of the expiring day, not more than a mile distant. It was resolved, without much formality, to give a clear sweep. Our steamer at once headed for the broad ocean. We bid farewell to Samana and set out for Puerto Plata.

CHAPTER XIII.

SAMANA BAY—ITS PHYSICAL FEATURES—THE PENINSULA—NOTES OF HISTORY.

OWING to the interposition of Luperon's piratical craft, and the unsettled condition of things on shore, I found it necessary to continue to Puerto Plata, there to disembark for an inland journey. While the opportunity offered, however, during our brief stay, I made minute observations of every feature within range of vision. On all sides spread the quiet waters of the bay, while the shore presented a varied landscape of towering peaks, beautiful valleys, and an unparalleled luxuriance of forest, flower, and fruit.

Standing in a northwesterly direction from Cape Engaño, the most eastern point of the island of San Domingo, and passing Cape Raphael, distant about fifty miles, we arrived off the entrance to the bay of

Samana. The coast was bold, and in many places rose perpendicularly out of the sea. The approach was well defined by high head-lands on the coast and mountain ranges in the interior. On the north side the conical crests of Azucar de Pilon, or Sugar Loaf Mountain, and La Montana del Diablo formed excellent land-marks. The entering channel lay on the north, along the peninsula.

At the eastern end of the peninsula were two capes, the most northern, Cape Cabron, a conspicuous white cliff, and Cape Samana, a bold rocky promontory near the channel. Between these two capes stretched a high perpendicular curtain of red cliffs with blue water under their very shadows. Penetrating the entrance between two less prominent projections—Vaca Point and Balandra Head—the shore was still bold and rocky. The latter head was of red formation, apparently sandstone. Passing Cape Samana the main bay had the appearance of a capacious bight sinking deep into the land. Upon closer examination, however, this sheet of water was well encircled and perfectly protected.

Between Cape Samana, on the north, and Cape Raphael, on the south, the mouth measured twenty-one miles northwest three-fourths north, reckoned from Cape Raphael. From this line, including the inner harbor as we may term it, the bay extended thirty miles, to the mouth of the Yuna river, one of the largest streams on the island, which enters the bay at the extreme western shore. The breadth of the bay, about mid-way its depth, from the town of Samana, on its northern, to Savannah la Mar, on its southern shore, was eight miles. Ten miles west of Cape Raphael, near Punta Jicaco, began a reef, which stretched northwestward to a number of islets, or rocks, called Cays (Keys) Pascual, Levantada, and Carenero, better known as the Bannister Cays. This reef protected the basin of the bay against the heavy seas, which otherwise, a gale from the north and east would send into it. The passage for the entrance and exit of vessels was thus contracted to one mile between Punta Cacao and Cay Pascual. In the middle of this channel was a small reef, marked on the charts, and called Jean Bart, having three and three-fourths fathom, or twenty-two feet of water. At other points not less than six fathoms or thirty-six feet of water was to be found, while a channel existed, well defined on the charts, showing nowhere less than eight fathoms or forty-eight feet. The reef Jean Bart lay northwest six cable lengths from the north point of Cay Pascual, which made it hazardous for sailing vessels of large size to leave with the prevailing sea breeze. It would therefore be advisable to stand out by the land breeze only.

Besides the principal bay there were several side anchorages, or coves (surge depots), extending into the land, the principal of which were Bahia de San Lorenzo and De las Perlas, on the southern shore, west of Savannah la Mar. This bay would form an excellent port. From its eastern point a shoal stretched about half a cable's length. The entrance to the bay gives from six and a half to eighteen fathoms.

In 1854, during negotiations then pending between the United States and the Dominican Republic in relation to the acquisition of the Bay of Samana, and a portion of the peninsula, General (then Captain) George B. McClellan was sent out by the United States Government to make some preliminary surveys. L. Howard Newman, passed midshipman United States Navy, on board the frigate Columbia, at the same time, coöperated in the survey, taking soundings. His official communication on the subject, dated August 5, 1854, says: "I have the honor to inform you that, entering the small bay between Points Lirio and Carenero from the eastward, you have ten and eleven fathoms water at the entrance and thereabout six fathoms in the middle of bay, gradually shoaling to the beach on the northward, and to the southward keeping about the same depth till you approach the reef. At the western extremity there is a small coral reef, or shoal, with from six to nine feet of water upon it, and around it about five or six fathoms. This, however, might be serviceable in constructing a wharf. The water at this end of the bay is deep enough for steamers of the first class, and a wharf of between two hundred and three hundred feet in length would allow vessels to lay alongside in four fathoms water. There is also a passage into this bay from the southward, between the small island of Carenero, Chequito, and the western point of the reef. This entrance has from seven to thirteen fathoms of water. To the westward of Point Lirio, in the Bahia de Clara, there is also an anchorage, and a convenient place for building a wharf, alongside of which vessels might lay in security.

"On the northward of the larger Bannister Cay there is a very good anchorage, the smaller cay and the shoal between the cays and the mainland forming a good breakwater against the heavy swell which might set in from the eastward. The depth of water varies from six to ten fathoms, and quite close to the beach there are four fathoms of water, so that in case it was found practicable to establish a small depot on the northwestern part of the cay, a wharf of little extent would afford facilities for coaling steamers. The approach to this latter anchorage is probably the least difficult of the three, although none present any very serious obstacles, particularly to vessels propelled by steam."

A letter from Commodore John Thomas Newton, commanding the home squadron, dated on board the United States flag-ship Columbia, Samana Bay, July 26, 1854, says: "I arrived here yesterday afternoon, entering this magnificent bay without meeting with any difficulty. We commenced watering the ships this morning from a delightful stream, half a mile distant from our anchorage. It is pure excellent water, and we managed to get it off with very little trouble. The surrounding country is beautiful as we view it from the ship. There is a fine anchorage in every direction."

The commodious character, as well as the remarkable advantages possessed by the Bay of Samana, may be judged from the fact that under the protection of the Cay Levantado, and communicating reefs, the largest fleet in the world would be perfectly secured from the sea and weather. This portion of the bay would answer admirably for an anchorage for ships out of commission, while the spacious bay outside of Levantado might be appropriated for vessels in active service. The shores around the bay are abrupt, and the largest vessels can lie in close. Around the Cay Levantado there is a sufficient depth of water to admit of vessels getting in so close as to communicate with the island by a common gangplank. The expansive surface of the bay would also also admit of manoeuvering vessels, with an abundance of room.

At the northeastern point of the Island of San Domingo from the mainland, along the northern shore of the Bay of Samana, stretches a narrow tongue of land thirty-two miles due east. The most eastern point of this peninsula, forming a bold and abrupt promontory, standing high out of the sea, is known as Cape Samana, or Cape Razon, called Cabo de San Feramo by Columbus. Formerly at the western extremity of the peninsula existed an open passage from sea to sea, used by the boatmen of Samana.

The isthmus is low. The lofty summits of the Monte Christi chain cease on approaching it, and rise again on the eastern bank of the Gran Estero, the western extremity of the peninsula. From west to east, as I have said, the peninsula is thirty-two miles.

The low land near the isthmus is about five miles wide, with the greatest breadth between Punta Balandra and Cape Cabron, where it is eleven miles. Samana is traversed by a central chain, rising highest at the eastern part. Pilon de Azucar, or Sugar Loaf mountain, near Cape Cabron, by measurement is 1,936 feet in height, and La Montano del Diablo, 1,300 feet. The area of Samana is 225 square miles, with a coast line of 95 miles. Several rivers find their outlets into the bay, and afford an abundance of fresh water for every purpose of the population, and for the use of vessels. The principal of these is the river Yuna. The Yuna rises in the central mountain chain on the highest peak of the Cibao, and, having passed close to the town of Cotuy, receives on its left the Camu. The Yuna has two mouths in the bay, and one northward into the Atlantic. In each there exists a bar with about three to four and a half feet of water. Its course is very tortuous, and, during the rainy season, the current is exceedingly strong. Boats formerly ascended the river some miles. The stream is navigable, inside the bars, for boats drawing four to five feet of water, as far as the junction of the Quaba. The Yuna, with a large population on its banks, would prove a valuable tributary of supplies, by native craft, to a population on the shores of Samana. The stream, with its branches, courses through the Royal Vega, (Royal Meadow,) one of the most fertile valleys in the world, and drains the mineral districts of Maymon and the pine forests of the Cibao. In 1867, the trade of the greater portion of the valley, which stretches from the Bay of Samana to Cotuy, on the Yuna, and to Conception, on the Camu, averaging eight miles in width, was carried on by native canoes of about two tons burden.

Towards the southward from the Yuna are the anchorages of Barranca Chica and Barranca Grande, not now used. The Naranjo river here enters the bay, passing under a hill of calcareous rock, through which it has forced an outlet. The central chain of mountains traversing the peninsula from west to east, in its geographical formation consists principally of mountain limestone schistose rocks, with veins of calcareous spar and sandstone. Quartz occurs frequently, and, at the eastern end of the peninsula, there is found an abundance of mica slates. A large quantity of fossil shells, in great variety, are met with. Near the rivulet of Almençon, veins of bituminous coal have been discovered. The specimens already produced indicate too much bitumen to be conveniently employed on steamers. The veins, however, have not been developed, and it is possible that a better quality exists. The coal deposits, according to Mr. Pennel, commence at a point called Los Robelas, about ten miles to the westward of the town of Santa Barbara, and crops out at intervals as far as Las Canitas, at the head of the bay, and, it is thought, extends to the base of the mountains separating the Royal Vega from the sea.

The soil of the peninsula of Samana, like all other portions of the island, is highly productive. It is covered with extensive forests of mahogany, espinello, caya, cavina, and other cabinet woods; roble and asaroble, suitable for ship building; capa, valuable for bottoms of vessels; and lignum vitæ. The soil and climate also produce indigo, cacao, cotton, and coffee. The present inhabitants are satisfied with cultivating yams, Indian corn, and fruits—chiefly bananas, plantains, pine-apples, oranges, mangoes, alligator pears, and cocoa-nuts—while from the jungle and the forest they gather, as the cravings of taste may dictate, other fruits in endless variety and inexhaustible abundance.

The bay of Samana abounds with fish, which is an important article of diet with the people on its shores. In spring, whales visit the adjacent sea. Near the mouth of the Yuna, oysters are found in large quantities. Aquatic birds visit the bay in great numbers—chiefly flamingoes, spoon-bills, scarlet ibis, snipe, and many other varieties.

The aboriginal people who dwelt upon the shores of the bay of Samana, were the Ciguayens, a fierce and warlike race, and are said by Columbus and others to have been very numerous. The population now consists of the descendants of Canarions or Islenos, the French refugees from Hayti, creoles from the same country, and the Spaniards from San Domingo. In 1824, another element was added in the arrival of a few free colored people from the American States of Pennsylvania and Maryland. About 300 of these people and their children are still living, the majority at Samana. They rank among the most intelligent and industrious on the island. In 1851, the population of the town of Samana was about 1,800 souls, of which nearly 300 were colored Americans. The chief commerce of Samana is with Turks Island—shipping provisions to that barren spot, and receiving in return quantities of salt.

.The small town of Santa Barbara is situated on the acclivities bordering a small bight on the north side of the bay, about six miles northwest of Cay Levantado. It was founded in 1756 by Don Francisco Rubray Peñarando, then Governor of San Domingo. On the southern shore, near the mouth of the Yabau, is the village of Savanna La Mar, containing a few hundred inhabitants.

CHAPTER XIV.

SAMANA BAY, AND THE WARS IN THE ANTILLES.

THE commodious bay of Samana was one of the earliest attractions of ancient Hispaniola. Since that time, its convenience of geographical position, from a strategic point of view, and the accommodations afforded by its well-sheltered and placid waters, have associated it with all the warlike operations of the Antilles.

After his discovery of the island, and giving some attention to a preliminary exploration of its coast, Columbus set out on his return to old Spain. In January, 1493, he passed a high head-land, which he named Cabo del Enamorado, (the Lovers' Cape,) now Cape Cabron. Farther eastward, he saw another, which he named Cabo San Feramo, now Cape Samana, which formed the most eastern point of the peninsula of the same name. Doubling this bold head-land, Columbus saw opened before him an expansive gulf, which he supposed to be an arm of the sea. A large native population, called Ciguayens, a fierce race, inhabited the shores. Columbus landed some of his men, with the desire to open friendly relations, when the natives assaulted the party. A lively fight ensued, in which the first blood between Europeans and the primitive people of the New World was shed. In consequence of this difficulty, Columbus named the portion of the bay nearest the scene of the fight, El Golfo de las Fleechas (the Gulf of Arrows.)

After passing three days here, Columbus departed for the Old World, carrying with him glowing accounts not only of the lands he had discovered but also of the great bay. In the subsequent operations of the Spanish, Samāna was frequently visited and was a place of refuge, in times of storm, for vessels sailing along the coast.

Fully appreciating the advantages of Samana, the Spanish Government established a settlement. A small town was built in 1756, together with a church dedicated to Santa Barbara. During these early scenes the strategic importance and value of Samana was fully recognized by the rival powers operating in the New World. In 1763, Count d'Estaing, as Governor General of the French island of Martinique, conceived the idea of securing the cession of the bay by Spain to France. These negotiations were suddenly broken off by the court of Madrid. The rival interests of the two powers on the island, were finally adjusted by defining the boundary between the French possessions in the west, and the Spanish, in the east of Hispaniola, according to the Treaty of Limits settled in 1777. By this arrangement, Samana remained in the hands of Spain.

When the insurrection of slaves broke out in the French part, a number of colonists and planters sought refuge in Spanish territory. Some of these fugitives joined the settlers at Samana. By the treaty of Basle, July 22, 1795, between France and Spain, the latter power ceded to France the eastern part of the island of San Domingo, in consideration of France giving up her conquests in the Pyrenees. Toussaint l'Ouverture, then general-in-chief of the forces, marched upon the city of San Domingo to take possession of the territory in the name of France.

In January, 1801, the tri-color waved over the whole island from Cape des Trois to Cape Engaño. Doubting Toussaint, the First Consul despatched General Le Clerc, his brother-in-law, to San Domingo with a formidable fleet of sixty war vessels and 30,000 troops. This fleet rendezvoused in the bay of Samana in January, 1802. Upon hearing of its arrival Toussaint, who was at the head of his army at the capital, mounted his horse, and with his customary energy galloped to the scene of this threatening intrusion. From the bold promontory of Cape Samana he contemplated in the broad bay at his feet the power of France concentrated for an invasion of his country. While thus reconnoitering the fleet, and the manœuvres of the vessels preparatory to their mission of blood and devastation, the negro warrior, for a moment, seemed struck with the magnitude of the war of oppression which must inevitably ensue. He exclaimed to the officers who had accompanied him: "We must perish; all France is coming to San Domingo. It has been decreed; it comes to take revenge and enslave the blacks." Samana now received a French garrison.

In 1808, when Napoleon assumed the throne of Spain, the Supreme Junta of Seville delegated Don Torribio Montes, Governor of Porto Rico, to incite the colonists of San Domingo against France. George III., by order in council July 4, 1808, made peace with Spain, and united with that power in a war against Napoleon. The Spanish population on the eastern coast of the island, headed by Don Juan Sanchez Ramirez, formerly commandante of Cotuy, rose, and at the battle of Palo Hincado defeated the French. Farrand, the French commander, shot himself in consequence of his misfortune.

An English squadron, consisting of three frigates and two brigs, from Jamaica, entered the bay of Samana in November of the same year, captured five vessels, and took Fort Santa Barbara. July 11, 1809, the city of San Domingo capitulated to the English fleet and General Sanchez.

Till the year 1821 Samana was little heard of. Excited by movements in Mexico and Venezuela, San Domingo declared herself independent of the mother country, and the insurgents hoisted the Columbian flag, calling the new State, Spanish Hayti. General Boyer, President of the Republic of Hayti, in 1822, made a sudden dash upon San Domingo. The new government, little prepared to defend itself against this unexpected attack, surrendered to Boyer, who annexed the country to French Hayti. In the same year Vice Admiral Jacob, with a French fleet of eleven vessels and 1200 troops, anchored in the Bay of Samana. The French landed, but the commander being informed by Boyer that upon any hostile act every Frenchman would be put to the sword, the French departed and abandoned whatever projects they may have had in view in regard to Samana.

CHAPTER XV.

NEGOTIATIONS OF THE UNITED STATES FOR THE ACQUISITION OF SAMANA.

IN 1853 the advantages possessed by the bay and peninsula of Samana for a naval station were brought to the attention of the United States Government. The plan suggested to Mr. Pierce, who was at that time President, was the allowance of a fixed annual rent in perpetuity for the use and occupation of a selected position, but with the proviso that the bay and peninsula should be declared a free port and neutral of war forever. In 1854 the United States frigate Columbia, Commodore Newton, conveyed a commissioner to San Domingo, with powers to negotiate for a naval depot at Samana. Captain, now General George B. McClellan, accompanied the mission. Leaving the commissioner at the capital of the island, the Columbia proceeded to Samana, where Captain McClellan made a survey of the coast on the north side from Port Balandra to Fort Santa Barbara, about six miles, and the Levantado and adjacent keys and reefs. He also laid out a desirable tract of land, to be appropriated in event of success as the site for the station on shore. Passed Midshipman L. Howard Newman also took soundings of the entrance to the bay. The results of the labors of both these officers, together with their views, I have already given. Everything was favorable to a speedy consummation of the important project. The engineers were enthusiastic in their admiration of the bay and its facilities for a naval and commercial depot. The bargain was about to be closed at a mere nominal price, when the delicate negotiations leaked out, and the British and French cabinets, alarmed at such a dangerous aggression, despatched at once two fleets, which concentrated before the capital of the island. The Dominican Government was made to understand that no foothold would be permitted to "such a dangerous power as the United States."

The Washington Cabinet summarily dropped all proceedings, not even supporting its negotiations with a dignified show of national pride. The commissioner returned to the United States, not in the best humor, as much from the calmness of taking the insult which had been offered to the nation, as from the failure of the project.

The question next came up in a new form. The Government having failed, it was proposed to establish a free port, on the principle and commercial basis of St. Thomas, with a United States mail and naval station on the site selected by McClellan. A plan was submitted to the consideration of some leading capitalists of New York, for the taking of Samana on a permanent lease, and sub-letting stations to the steam companies of any or all parts of the world. The capitalists and the Dominican government came into the arrangement, but made a condition that the United States should agree, by a formal treaty with the Dominican authorities, to recognize the free and neutral status of Samana. This proposition was submitted to Mr. Buchanan, then President of the United States, in the early part of his administration. At the same time it was proposed, by private parties, that all individual interests would be withdrawn, if the Government preferred acting on its own account. Buchanan at first hesitated, but was at length induced to inaugurate anew measures looking to the acquisition.

While the United States was exhausting time and

patience in stupid delays, Spain loomed up, seriously alarmed at the fresh dangers besetting her. The Castilian envoy at Washington denounced the project as an act of war against his sovereign. The movers in the scheme were set down by the bewildered and alarmed plenipotentiary as Cuban filibusters, and the free port of Samana was in reality nothing more than a harbor and base of operations for revolutionists of the "ever faithful isle." (?) The press of France and Spain kept up a lively assault upon "the designs on Samana." The United States Government again receded—an evidence of administration by weak hands and weaker heads.

In 1859 the United States was advised of the hostile designs of Spain against San Domingo, and again pressed the completion of the Samana question. While Mr. Buchanan was revolving the question in his unsettled brain, the Dominican Republic expired. A Spanish army occupied the city of San Domingo, and a Spanish navy closely watched the coast. Under the new administration of Mr. Lincoln, Seward left a wide field open to Spain by dropping the whole question. The Monroe doctrine, which he managed by force of circumstances to a more successful issue in Mexico, he entirely ignored in San Domingo. Spain, taking advantage of the importance of

Samana, as developed in the negotiations of the United States for its possession, turned her attention to the establishment of a naval depot upon the very site laid out by McClellan in 1854, and planned extensive fortifications to make it, with the assistance of art, what it was by nature, the Gibraltar of the Antilles. The timely uprising of the Dominican people, and the restoration of the republican constitution and flag, defeated the plans of Spain, and saved the United States from having in the very line of her commerce in the Gulf of Mexico and the Caribean sea a stronghold in the hands of a European nation.

The return of the legitimate form of government on the island opened afresh the question of Samana. The Dominican government lost no time, and in 1864 despatched an envoy to Washington to offer the bay and peninsula of Samana at a nominal rent, on the basis of the original proposition. The envoy presented himself, and in return for the warm impulses which actuated the steps taken by the Dominican government, Mr. Seward uncourteously refused to receive the envoy, or even to listen to him unofficially. Several Senators were appealed to, and the advantages to accrue from the acquisition were so evident, and met with so much favor, that

Mr. Seward, probably as an offset, at this moment began his negotiations with the Danish Court for the sterile peaks, diminutive harbor, and undeveloped earthquakes of St. Thomas. At the same time the Secretary kept up a sort of awkward coquetry with San Domingo. The Dominican Cabinet, being repeatedly put off, in turn exhibited great surprise at the sudden ardor of the American Minister, and doubting the sincerity of his intentions, in view of the negotiations for St. Thomas, declined to treat. Again the question dropped.

In November, 1866, the negotiations were once more seriously opened between the two governments: President José Maria Cabral was in power and looked favorably upon the prospects of a closer union between the United States and San Domingo. After the repeated disgrace to which our flag and nation had been subjected, by the conduct and common worthlessness of some of the commercial agents, sent out by the United States, to represent American interests, Mr. J. Somers Smith, a gentleman of character and social standing, was put in charge. Mr. Smith had had many years' experience as Consul in Spain, and was therefore fitted for the position. To him the new propositions were made for a lease of the coal mines of Samana and the Levantado and Carenero Keys. These facts Mr. Smith communicated to the department at Washington. Upon this letter Frederick Seward, Assistant Secretary of State, arrived at San Domingo, in January, 1867, in the United States steamer Gettysburg. Negotiations were at once opened, and continued five or six days. The representatives of the two governments could come to no terms. The Dominican representatives asked a joint occupation, which, on the part of the United States, was declined, on the ground that that government would hold no property in conjunction with another power. Here the question again terminated. The very next month, however, Mr. Smith succeeded in consummating the first treaty between the two Republics, termed "A general convention of amity, commerce, and extradition," which was exchanged October 5, 1867. This treaty was modeled on the plan of those with Venezuela and Hayti.

In February, of the same year, Mr. Smith received, from the State Department, the full powers of a commissioner to negotiate the Samana matter. In August of the same year Hayti, becoming alarmed and evidently jealous of the benefits which would accrue to the Dominicans in the event of the United States possessing Samana, sent to the Dominican authorities a treaty, which had in view nothing more than the prevention of the alienation of territory, and a mutual agreement to put a stop to the revolutionary movements constantly fitting out in one country against the other.

Upon the downfall of Cabral and the accession of Buenaventuro Baez, the present President, Samana once more became the topic of discussion. This was in March, 1868. The proposition was again to lease, to which the United States replied that it was not then willing to lease territory from any foreign power.

Little, if any credit, belongs to the United States Government for the efforts, at least, to secure to the people a possession which, in her new relations with the rest of the world, would evidently prove very advantageous. All the negotiations, hitherto had upon the Samana question, failed because the government never came out with a boldly-defined proposition and with the material to back it. But the course pursued had, at least, the appearance, in case of emergency, of a contemplated violation of faith. In such action a revolution would have been inevitable, for the failure would have been thrown before the population as a sufficient ground of complaint. In a successful and sincere consummation of the transfer, in fee, for a small consideration, there would have been a unanimous expression of approbation on the part of that portion of the population desiring peace.

A reference to a general map of the chain of islands, separating the Gulf of Mexico from the Caribbean Sea, will at once suggest the importance of the geographical position of the Island of San Domingo, in the Antilles, with relation to its value as a strategic point, either in naval or commercial operations. It stands between the two principal Spanish possessions in America—Cuba and Porto Rico—and controls the English island of Jamaica and the Windward islands to the eastward. Samana bay and peninsula, as an easily accessible and commodious station on the island, is certainly the central point at which all the advantages of a position in the tropical regions are to be realized, Its contiguity to the United States, and other points of significance, may be judged by the following table of distances, either estimated or official:

	MILES.
From Samana to New York,	1,300
" " " Porto Rico, (western end,)	60
" " " Turk's Island,	165
" " " Puerto Plata, San Domingo,	110
" " " Island of Saona,	100
" " " San Domingo City,	240

	MILES.
From Samana to the Spanish Main,	600
" " " to Aspinwall,	1,000
" " " Key West, Fla.,	800
" northwest end of San Domingo Island to Cuba,	60

It will be seen that steamers, stationed in the bay, would have convenient access to all the surrounding islands and coasts, and for purposes of trade or as a coaling station, the position is admirable. The coal mines of Samana are as yet undeveloped, and therefore nothing can be said of their probable utility. With such flattering indications it is still encouraging that this valuable and indispensable material, in modern navigation, will be found in quantity and quality to answer every purpose. I have already alluded to the unexampled fertility of the adjacent country, its excellent building material of limestone and sandstone, and valuable and inexhaustible forests of wood for cabinet and domestic uses and ship building, its streams of pure water, its vegetable productions, its animal life. These natural resources will certainly attract and give subsistence to a teeming population, and lead to a community of wealth, enterprise, and prosperity, unequaled in the tropics—a sort of outpost of the great republic of the North.

Nature has also performed wonders for the defence of the position, which, by the assistance of human ingenuity, could be rendered impregnable.

The destiny of all the islands of the Antilles is American. The influence of American institutions, at least in the Western hemisphere, daily becomes more deeply felt, and as time moves on we observe its mysterious operations more openly exhibited. As the model of republican greatness, the small powers of America look to the United States for the examples which shall direct and govern their development of new forms of government, independent, and on the principles of liberty. The responsibility of the United States is, therefore, great. There is a necessity for a policy distinct from that employed in relations with the concerns of the Old World. A policy, American and Republican, adapted to the demands of a people and territories united with us in a community of national aspiration and an identity of destiny. All these considerations demand, as a preliminary step, the presence of the republican flag of the United States, and nowhere could it better be planted than in the Bay of Samana, which would at once become "the American Gibraltar of the Antilles."

CHAPTER XVI.

COTABANAMA, THE GIANT KING.

ON the tongue of land, bounded on the north by the Bay of Samana and the Yuna, and on the west by the Ozama, existed a brave and warlike people. Their incessant conflicts with the Caribs had developed a martial skill not visible in any of the other inhabitants of the island. Four of the native kings had already been deposed, and were ruthlessly butchered, or sent in chains to the dungeons of Old Spain. Cotabanama, Cacique of the Higuey, alone remained.

The Spaniards, having gained undisputed control of the greater portion of island, now concluded to complete their dominion by the subjugation of Higuey.

Cotabanama was, according to cotemporary authorities, a man of huge proportions. He was taller by far than the tallest, and measured a yard from shoulder to shoulder. His bow was too powerful to be used by any of his subjects. The arrows were three-pronged and tipped with bone. All his weapons were those of a powerful giant. Under the lead of such a king the Higueyans had triumphed in all their encounters with enemies of their own race.

A small vessel was seized within the king's dominions, and the crew slaughtered, out of revenge for the death of a cacique, who had been torn to pieces by dogs.

As soon as this act was communicated to the Spaniards, at their capital, a force of four hundred men was organized and sent into Cotabanama's country. The king rallied his warriors for a stubborn defence. The Spaniards, in all their conflicts with the natives, had nowhere experienced such determined opposition and display of military skill. A single Indian, it is said, engaged two mounted cavaliers. He was pierced through the body, but kept on fighting, until he fell dead with all the weapons of the Spaniards in his possession.

Against the terrible engines of war brought into the contest the warriors of Cotabanama found it impossible to cope. After a stubborn struggle, in which the invaders had little occasion to rejoice, the Indians were defeated. This disaster was attended with the same diabolical atrocities that had been visited upon the subjects of the neighboring kings. The people took refuge in the various caves of the country. The island of Saona, where the war had its origin, was the object of special and even more terrible punishment.

When quiet was again restored Cotabanama visited the Spanish camp. His remarkable physical proportions struck all with amazement. The admiration of Juan de Esquibel, a man of rare prowess, was so completely captivated that he exchanged names with the giant Cacique.

The peace, which had been effected with so much bloodshed, and followed by such persistent atrocity, was but short-lived. During the administration of Ovando it became necessary to suppress a new uprising of the brave Higuayans. Nothwithstanding the difficulties which impeded the progress of the Spaniards, in following an enemy in a country covered with mountains, Cotabanama soon found himself not only defeated, but his sceptre hopelessly fallen from his hands.

The cruelty of the Spaniards, if possible, surpassed in fiendish ingenuity that which had attended their first victory. Thirteen of the leading men of the country were hanged, out of revenge, they said, for the Saviour and the twelve apostles.

Juan de Esquibel, who had on a former occasion paid a high tribute of respect for Cotabanama, was now in command. He declared that the country could never be subjugated until the Cacique king was taken.

When all had gone against him, Cotabanama, with his family, withdrew to the island of Soana, two leagues from the coast. In the centre of this island was a labyrinth of caves, situated in the heart of a deep and dark forest. Here the king took refuge, accompanied only by his wife and children, and a few faithful adherents. When the flight of the Cacique became known, Esquibel, in person, with fifty trusty men, set out in the night, bent upon his capture. The Spaniards landed on the island under the shadow of precipitous rocks. Cotabanama's scouts, constantly posted to give the alarm should the hated and inflexible strangers pursue, failed to discover their approach. Two of the Cacique's men were taken. One was instantly put to death. The other was forced to lead the way to the retreat of their chief.

While hastening into the dark forests, the Spaniards came to a point where the roads diverged. All, except only Juan Lopez, pursued the same road to the right. A foot-path, merely, penetrated the compact and impenetrable surroundings of forest-trees and shrubbery. Suddenly, in a narrow pass, Lopez found himself confronting twelve stalwart warriors. Though powerful in body, and dexterous in the use of defensive and offensive weapons, a less stout-hearted soldier would have beat a hasty retreat. The savage warriors had it in their power to despatch the daring Spaniard on the spot. Lopez, undaunted at the superiority of numbers, boldly demanded of the leading warrior where was his chief. Overawed by his air of confident strength, the terrified and surprised natives replied that he was behind. "Then let him pass," demanded Lopez. Cotabanama came forward. The enraged Cacique was about to drive an arrow from his powerful bow into the body of Lopez, when the courageous soldier rushed upon his giant antagonist. The Cacique warded off the blow of the sword, and the two grappled. The contest was fierce. Both combatants were of unsurpassed physical strength. The Cacique was, however, too much for Lopez. He had his powerful grasp upon his throat, and attempted to strangle him. The noise made in the struggle brought the rest of the Spaniards to the spot. The warriors of the Cacique, intimidated by the boldness of Lopez, had already deserted. It was now but the work of a moment to overpower the Cacique. He was securely bound, and was closely guarded, while Esquibel, with a few companions, set out for the secret cave. But the wife and children of the Cacique were gone. It was in vain they searched for them. Never after did the relentless invaders hear of them. The Spaniards could not restrain their ferocity. It was proposed to execute the chief on the spot. A pyre was built in the shape of a gridiron. Upon this fiendish instrument of torture the heroic Cotabanama was to be slowly broiled to death. Before they had put their atrocious purposes in force, their minds were diverted in favor of a greater glorification over the tragic fate of the Cacique of the Higuey. It was decided to convey him to the capital in chains. Upon arriving there, he was ignominiously hanged. Thus expired the last of the five native sovereigns of Hayti.

Now ensued a scene of diabolical cruelty, sufficient to touch the sympathies of the most hardened. In a few years the island was almost depopulated of its primitive inhabitants. No more the areyots of the natives were heard recounting in song the deeds of their people; the sacred palm groves were deserted — all was ruin and desolation!

CHAPTER XVII.

ARRIVAL AT PUERTO PLATA—THE GOVERNOR OF THE CITY—FAREWELL TO THE TYBEE—OFF FOR THE INTERIOR.

THE morning after the expeditious and summary departure of the steamer from the bay of Samana found us anchored in the small, but well-protected, harbor of Puerto Plata. I proposed here to leave the steamer and perform a trifle of land navigation. Having left my heavier parcels at the capital, I was little encumbered with baggage. Bidding farewell to Delanoy and the purser, Vannard, as well as to the companions of a most delightful voyage, I took a small boat for the shore. Reaching the shallow water, I was transferred to a bullock-cart, which, having just discharged a load of logwood on a lighter, drove alongside. In this rude vehicle, accompanied by an ebony servant, my valise, an umbrella, and a cane, I made my debut in the city of Puerto Plata.

I was not long in making my way to an uninviting caravansary termed a hotel. Having ordered dinner immediately, I sallied forth to take an introductory view of the place, to present several letters of introduction furnished me by the President, and to lay out a programme for my future movements. I called upon the commercial agent of the United States, with whom I had a brief conversation, and at the same time had my passports properly signed and stamped. In company with the agent, I delivered the letters which had been given me, commending me to the consideration and courtesy of El General Gobenador Juan Neuzi, Señor Don José Maria Orzens, Adm'r de Hacienda de Puerto Plata, and Señor Don Ignacio Gonzales. The governor received me with the utmost kindness. He was a pure black, stout in person, but very affable in manner. His office was in an extremely small and unpretending building, which I considered a very striking indication of the extremely impoverished condition of the government. After a conversation of some minutes, explaining the object of my visit and what my movements were to be, I had my passport countersigned by the governor, and left him to his glory.

I now repaired to the establishment of a merchant and shipper, to which place I was introduced by the commercial agent. The warehouse was a commodious stone building, stuccoed. In great stacks were ceroons of tobacco ready to be shipped to Germany. Several natives were engaged in repacking and weighing a new lot of the "weed" that had just come in. Besides with tobacco, the building was well crammed with a supply of other articles of export, as well as a large amount of imported goods, for which there was a demand in the country. Outside the building, quite a crowd of persons were busily engaged in unloading the cargoes of tobacco, brought down from the Santiago region on the backs of ponies, donkeys, or bullocks. I was satisfied in a very short time that there was little necessity of spending any time in Puerto Plata. Accordingly, I commenced looking about me for some means of transportation to Santiago de los Caballeros, about nineteen leagues in the interior by the road. I found, much to my disgust, that there were but two spare horses in the town. One was owned by an elderly woman, who proposed taking a little trip to the interior herself. The other was without any saddle, it being the custom of the country to furnish a horse without saddle or bridle. Before going any further,

I returned to the hotel, and fortified myself with a quantity of food, badly cooked, and a certain cause of intestine commotion.

After dinner, I again called on my merchant friend and stated the impossibility of my getting a horse in the town, and my anxiety to be on the road. He consoled my uneasiness by saying that he could arrange matters, and, if no better opportunity offered, he could "ship" me with one of the packing parties returning to Santiago. I told him it mattered not how I got there, so I was not compelled to lose any time in inactivity. With this comforting information, I set out to take a look at the town. As there was little to see but ruin, the task was not a severe one.

Puerto Plata is one of the early Spanish towns, laid out to accommodate the trade of the northern coast. It was founded some time about the commencement of the seventeenth century, for in 1606 it was proscribed for smuggling. When the Spaniards were forced to evacuate the island they completely destroyed the place. To-day the ruins show that Puerto Plata, in the day of its prosperity, was by no means insignificant. The modern town has a population of about two thousand inhabitants, a mixture of Spanish, Germans, French, and two or three Americans, together with a large preponderance of blacks and mulattoes, native born. It has been entirely rebuilt, hardly a single structure having escaped destruction.

Puerto Plata is now the only open harbor on the north side of the island. The proceeds of the custom-house are the main source of the revenue of the government. Though the town is small and uninviting, it has a well protected harbor. The town depends almost entirely on Santiago, and the comparatively populous districts in the vicinity, for its business. Of this interior city, it is the seaport for the shipment of the tobacco, and other productions, gathered in the Vega, and thence transported on the backs of animals down to the coast.

I was told that practically all the tobacco shipments were to Hamburg, and that the crops of 1868–'69 would reach one hundred thousand quintals, or ten millions pounds.

The country around Puerto Plata is mountainous, though it possesses a soil of remarkable fertility. The population, however, is sparse, and as a consequence little is produced of any value, farther than supplying the inhabitants of the town.

There was great talk of a railroad from Santiago, to terminate at Puerto Plata. Concesssions had been granted, but the instability of the Government was likely to prevent very speedy progress in the necessary enterprise.

A short distance west of Puerto Plata are still to be found the ruins of Isabella, the first Christian city built upon the western hemisphere. The place was founded by Columbus himself upon his second visit to the island, having been driven into the harbor by stress of weather while in search of a suitable site with accommodations for vessels. The place is now overgrown with forests of mahogany and *campeche*. The pillars of the church, portions of the king's store-house, and the building supposed to have been occupied by Columbus, the small fortress, and a few barely visible traces of the walls surrounding the place, are all that is left to mark the spot. The site was unhealthy, and was abandoned, after the transfer of the seat of government on the island, to the mouth of the Ozama.

After I had satisfied myself that the town possessed little to invite a stranger to tarry long within its limits, I strolled off along the bay shore. The steamer was just passing out of the harbor. Naturally upon parting with companions of travel a transient sensation of regret passes through the mind. But I must admit that I saw the steamer starting upon her homeward journey with deeper feelings than those of regret. I was now left to my own resources to pick up acquaintances, and to make friends. I could not help indulging in a momentary longing to be once more upon the water. I walked back to the establishment of my merchant friend, and found that all necessary arrangements had been made to enable me to reach Santiago. In a country without roads, and the means of transportation not very abundant, it required no little diplomacy to get hold of an odd horse, or more correctly to get the possessors of animal locomotion to come to a favorable consideration on any terms whatever.

The animal placed at my disposal was not the most spirited I had ever backed. It was a mild-tempered roan, with a full complement of sound limbs, and one of a "pack" which had arrived at the town that morning, laden with ceroons of tobacco. The peon in charge was an intelligent fellow, and evidently indulging in a sufficient amount of commiseration, in view of my situation, agreed to deliver me and my baggage at Santiago at the very reasonable sum of five dollars.

I felt considerably animated at this favorable prospect, and announced that I was ready to start at any time. Having procured sufficient supplies to serve me on the journey, and seeing that they were stowed away with my valise in the *arganna*, on the peon's horse, I thanked my merchant friend for his courtesy, indulged in the traveler's compliment of inviting to call if he ever came to the United States, mounted my roan, and followed by a troop of quadrupeds and swarthy natives, set out on the first stage of my journey to the interior.

CHAPTER XVIII.

TRAVELING UNDER DIFFICULTIES—AN UNIQUE ESTABLISHMENT—A MOTLEY RETINUE ASCENDING THE MONTE CHRISTI RANGE—SCENES ON THE ROAD.

DID not consider my start by any means propitious of a very convenient or comfortable journey over the seventy leagues I would be compelled to traverse before reaching once more the luxuries of Mons. Auguste's hotel. I was consoled, however, before leaving Puerta Plate, by the intelligence that I would experience no embarrassment, at Santiago, in making very satisfactory arrangements for the rest of the distance.

The cardinal virtue necessary to the successful accomplishment of the journey I was about inaugurating, considering the circumstances, was patience. The locomotion of the animals took no heed of time.

It seemed to concern the peon little, judging from his manner, whether he completed his journey the next day, or the next week. I had no voice in the matter, and with philosophical resignation turned my mind and attention to surrounding scenes. In the first place, I contemplated myself. I found this an amusing subject. Between me and the back of my horse was a rude pack-saddle made out of dried banana leaves and small reeds, put together in two rolls, about eight inches in diameter and four feet in length. The two ends were sprung so as to meet, leaving an elliptical opening in the centre. The two ends were turned up. Into this sort of trough I had been deposited, and with the one end running up in front and the other behind, I had no occasion to feel uneasy about falling out. The saddle surmounted a heavy mat, of native work, which was not less than three inches thick, and extended from the withers close up to the horses' crupper. My feet dangled loosely by the animal's side. This inconvenience was afterwards remedied by an improvised pair of rope stirrups. Another piece of rope, over the animal's nose, answered the purpose of a bridle.

I did not inwardly complain of my mount, for the satisfaction of being on the road was sufficient consolation. I had hardly cleared the outskirts of the town, than I found myself surrounded by a highly picturesque and miscellaneous escort of peons, including a few boys and girls, mounted on horses of various sizes, donkeys and bullocks of divers conditions and infirmities. The peons each wore a pair of pantaloons and a straw hat, and a few had shirts. The women wore a kind of smock, of coarse material, extending a short distance below the knees. The younger boys and girls were entirely naked. The men wore the inevitable *machete*. Occasionally drawing the rusty blade from its ponderous and primitive scabbard, with a wild shout they would flourish it with considerable energy, hewing large swathes of foliage from the profuse vegetation by the way, or at intervals allowed it to descend broadside upon their animals' rump, with a peculiarly emphatic, enlivening, and accelerating effect.

The road for a short distance ran over a stretch of low country, covered with groves of palm and cocoa-nut trees. The smaller vegetation covered the soil with a tangled mass of green of every variety of shade, and an infinite diversity of leaf. In the midst of this luxuriance of nature the *bohios*, or palm-thatched huts of the natives were to be seen here and there peeping through the foliage of shrubbery and flowers.

After crossing this belt, not more than a mile in width, the road struck the base of the first range of the series of high mountains which constitute the northern or Monte Christi spur of the Cibao chain. This range has its point of departure at Cape Samana, at the eastern extremity of the peninsula of the same name, and after disappearing in the isthmus which extends from the bay to the Atlantic ocean, across the western end of the peninsula, rises again, and follows the line of the northern coast of the island, entirely disappearing in the vicinity of the town of Monte Christi. The whole range possesses a soil of rare fertility, and is covered with endless forests of mahogany, *campeche*, lignum vitæ, and other valuable woods. Mountain streams drain the slopes on the north, finding their outlet into the broad bosom of the Atlantic. On the south, after coursing through beautiful savannas, they become tributary to the Yuna, which disembogues into the tranquil waters of Samana, or fall into the Yaque, winding, like a silver cord, down the basin of an extensive valley, and reach the ocean through the western portals of the Cibao.

An avenue of carpeted green, at least eighty feet in width, cut through the towering forest, could be traced ascending to the loftiest summits in front.

From all appearances, at a distance, this opening looks as if it were the remains of an ancient highway. Experience proved this to be a delusion. The avenue which, at a distance, presented such a gratifying prospect of an easy journey, I found fearfully cut up by bridle-paths, worn deep into the soil, as if they had been the lines of the traffic of centuries, and crossed each other in labyrinthine confusion. At places the road was covered with small stones; at other points was wet and slippery. At times the road-path wound among boulders, then through narrow passages, beneath and between overhanging and rocky walls, or over detached rocks of such dimensions, that it would be thought, except after the experience of a trial, impossible to surmount them astride any animal lacking such convenient accessories of climbing as a complement of claws and a stout forearm.

As, with my motley retinue, I penetrated deeper into the forest and ascended higher upon the acclivities of the mountain, the road seemed to be rapidly approximating a perpendicular. Frequently the ascent was so precipitous that the attitude of my body was thrown considerably out of line, and not unfrequently I found my nose almost poised midway between my horse's ears, while the other extremity was exposed to the receding view. It resembled a new posture for the study of a horseman, riding all-fours. I found myself constantly losing ground. It frequently required considerable manual strength and dexterity, not counting the risk of pulling out my horse's mane, to keep from describing a retrograde movement over the crupper. I thus found for myself an abundance of mental and physical occupation, in meeting the various requisite postures known and unknown, in the code of expert and artistic horsemanship. My ragged escort sat unconcernedly upon their animals, at intervals breaking out in their mountain airs, a mixture of wild cadence and bad Spanish, with a lusty vigor, banishing all present care or thought of the morrow. I often, on the journey, watched their contented spirit, by way of relief, with cogitations instructive of much philosophy and lessons worthy of imitation in a higher sphere. Although their condition was but a few steps above the brute, with which their lives were associated, they have the solace of a satisfied lot and an existence knowing only the simplest rudiments of human desire. From morning until night, the dark defiles and crowning elevations of the mountain were enlivened by their songs. At times these rude efforts consisted of single parts, and again of a musical dialogue or colloquy. The leader would probably lead off and sing a few measures. The man bringing up the rear, probably fifty yards off, would respond. After repeating this a few times, others would take it up, until all joined in unison in a wild chorus. At last I had reached the crest of the first range. I here halted for a few moments to take a retrospective view of my route and of the region I had left behind. Far in the dim distance rolled the blue waters of the Atlantic, nearer broke into view the town and harbor of Puerto Plata, standing out in trembling miniature, over tree tops and intervening gorges and forest. The "*bohios*" of the natives, embowered in nature's profusion, were but faintly visible, and sometimes were marked only by a circling thread of smoke, ascending lazily upon the motionless atmosphere.

But my suite were not disposed to such sentimental digressions. As the hours were fast running their course into night, I yielded to the evident spirit of uneasiness which prevailed. My escort, I perceived, however, had no disposition to desert me, for with some small accessions in the way of voluntary recruits, I was very faithfully attended throughout the journey.

CHAPTER XIX.

A HARD DAY'S JOURNEY—BAD ROADS—HOSPITALITY—
A FEAST—THE WIDOW OF AN AMERICAN NEGRO.

NATURE'S daily performance of very suddenly vaulting into darkness found me still on the road. As I had set out with the resolution of leaving everything to the peon in charge, I followed on without any attempt at interference with regard to halting for the night. It was not long after the thoughts of resting had occurred to me, that I was brought suddenly to a halt in front of a *palisa*, or staked fence. The peon entered the enclosure, and, with little negotiation, came to an arrangement. Notifying me, I also entered, followed in single file by my suite. I was conducted, by the dim light of a pine stick, around the building occupied by the family, to a spare and isolated structure a few feet off, which, at day-light the next morning, I found to be a store-house, well stocked with fruits, rude implements of husbandry, native pack-saddles, mats, and an almost endless variety of articles entirely new to me. I dismounted according to orders. By this time the pine torch had burnt itself out. By means of the dubious light of the stars, I groped my way in. After the animals had been cared for, which consisted in turning them loose to provide for themselves, a small fire was built by the peons and burrequeros. My hammock, that indispensable companion of travel in San Domingo, was swung. After the confinement of a sea-voyage, I was little inured to the severe exertion I was now indulging in, and, consequently, felt very much fatigued. After a frugal meal from the stock of supplies I had brought with me, and lighting a Dominican cigar, I threw myself into my hammock. It was not long before my cigar was discarded for the resuscitating influence of a sound sleep.

The next morning, I awoke before day-light, and, indulging in a more deliberate breakfast, found myself on the way by sun-rise. The road, during the entire day, lay over a succession of mountain ranges and across intervening valleys, knee deep with mud and water from the daily rains of the season. At places, the descent of steep declivities was not the least dangerous feat to perform, particularly where the rain had left the surface wet and insecure. In the valleys it was frequently necessary to leave the road, though these necessary departures apparently afforded no better travel than in the main highway. In addition, the narrow path, running through thick shrubbery, was exceedingly wet, and the net-work of roots coursing through the soil, frequently dragged the horse into the mud. Progress, under such circumstances, was a question of patience and perseverance, rather than expedition and ill temper. The road was a curiosity of engineering skill. It appeared to me as if those who laid it out must have lost themselves in the forest, and wandered about for several days oblivious of their destination. An idea of the force of this statement may be gathered when I say that, although it is very nearly sixty miles by the road, it is only sixteen in a line, between Puerto Plata and Santiago de los Caballeros. During the day I passed through Altamira, a small village of thirty or forty native hamlets. Occupying a high position, the view from that point was remarkably fine and extensive in mountain and valley scenery.

Late in the afternoon, while rounding a bold promontory in the Campo Diego and abutting far out into the plain, I got a first glimpse of Santiago de los Caballeros, which lay at a distance of not less than ten miles. A broad valley, at least twelve miles in width, stretched from mountain to mountain, and, on a beautiful rise in the surface, lay this ancient city. In descending from the mountains, the road followed a deep, dark, and narrow gorge between two parallel ranges. At some places, I followed in the bed, or on the sandy margin, of a stream, there being no greater a width than from twelve to twenty feet from boulder to boulder of the mountains on either side. This part of the journey was wild and interesting. In a distance of a mile, in the gorge, I crossed back and forth, over the same stream, seven times. I was afterwards informed, when mentioning the fact, that there were thirty-three streams between the two cities. After leaving the gorge and debouching upon the plain, the road became broad, and showed signs of immense numbers of animals passing over it. During the day, I had an opportunity of forming some idea of the large traffic between the interior city and the entrepot on the coast. We were constantly meeting droves of from fifteen to twenty donkeys, horses, or bullocks, and sometimes but the solitary burro and his burroquero, all tending towards the sea-port.

The great majority of the animals were laden with tobacco, from two to three hundred pounds weight, according to size, condition, and strength. The tobacco was swung across the animal's back, the load being divided in two parts and placed in *argannas*, or native panniers, woven out of the palm leaf.

We were often detained on the way, in narrow places, to allow the loaded packs to pass.

By the time I had left the mountains darkness had again set in, and a second night on the road was inevitable, and preferable too, as I had no desire to enter the town thus late. My peon conducted me a short distance along the main road, and then branching off into the thicket, after a dark and dubious ride, brought me out at another native hut.

I found my peon and the female of the establishment were old and intimate friends. The landlord it seems had been removed, but a short time before, by grim death. I was here accommodated with the best the place afforded. I was not as fatigued by the journey as I was the night before, nothwithstanding the day's travel had been continuous and severe. I found my widowed hostess almost annoying in her attentions. She refused to allow my own hammock to be swung, but produced one of her own, a new one, which she insisted I should use. I diplomatically yielded. The hammock was swung under a projecting thatched roof, which answered the double purpose of a porch and a drying place for tobacco.

While these preliminary ceremonies were going on children made their appearance. I felt a strong inclination to drop at once into the inviting folds of my snow-white hammock; but after so much unexpected courtesy I considered that etiquette demanded I should delay my departure for the regions of sleep.

A half an hour had hardly elapsed when a lad of about twelve years of age, addressing me in my own tongue, invited me to eat something. I could not well refuse, notwithstanding very threatening inward indications of revolt. I was conducted across an intervening space between the main hamlet and a structure, made up of a thatched roof, supported on four forked poles.

My hostess was in a high state of delight, and to add to her own joy on the occasion sent round to her neighbors, inviting them to join her in doing the honors.

Greatly to my surprise I found I was set down for a native feast. A dozen females were seated about on stones and logs. Several men were also in the group. All were black except my hostess, who was a mulatto of comely face and person. I must admit that I was greatly disconcerted at this quiet, unexpected, and extraordinary treatment. My hostess having beckoned me to a seat, I took the one pointed out to me, which consisted of a curious root, fashioned into a very comfortable chair. I was planted also, immediately, in front of a small fire, and in greater proximity than the atmosphere would naturally prompt one to fall into.

The guests now gathered around, and it was but a moment before I was enveloped in a cloud of dusky beauty and fashion, and an atmosphere not very ethereal. My olfactories were sorely pressed at the sociability of my friends. All the females had on their best clothes, which, though primitive in style, and sparse in quantity, gave them quite a neat appearance. The men were not so particular, and looked as if they had not indulged in a change since the beginning of the year. The children were entirely naked.

My hostess took a seat on a low block of wood at my feet and near the fire. A number of plantains lying on the ground, a few in the ashes baking, and others stewing, gave premonitory symptoms of what diet I might expect. The hostess began poking the baked plantains out of the ashes with a stick. Having found a nice large one, she broke it in two, and putting the halves on a piece of a China plate, handed them to me. I accepted, of course, with *mil gracias*. The rest of the company were also provided by taking the plantains in their fingers. It was the severest trial of the day to dispose of this first course. Native food is a thing to which all travelers should accustom themselves, but between the dry, tasteless, pithy interior of a plantain and a very dry corncob, I could find no distinction. I managed, however, to force a few pieces out of sight by resorting to a slight indulgence in "Dominican" as a stimulator in getting these obstructions out of my throat, where they lodged in the very beginning. The next course was a supply of stewed plantains. A frightful quantity was passed over on my plate. The rest took their's in calabash bowls. As this was more moist, I found great assistance in gravitating, nearer the seat of digestion, the baked pieces which had gone in before.

I was now rejoiced to find that there was no more eating to be done. I at once made myself at ease by cultivating my hostess and entertaining her nude offspring. I struck up a conversation with the lad who had attracted my attention by his acquaintance with my native tongue. I became, very soon, much interested. The lad, though but twelve years of age, was unusually bright, and from him I obtained a great deal of interesting family information. He told me his father came from the United States, and the State of Pennsylvania. He did not know when, but it was long ago. His mother, he said, was a native of San Domingo. His father often talked about the great country from which he came, and tried to teach all his children to speak his own language. His father had died but a few months before. The mother was very much pleased when I said that I was glad to see the family of an American; that the children were Americans because their father was.

In their listless lives the natives care little of time, and lolling about in the heats of the day, their nights are, as occasion offers, devoted to recreation and pleasure, This opportunity was an extraordinary one, and they evidently had made up their minds to prolong its advantages for enjoyment.

My peon and the burrequeros had long stowed themselves away in another part of the structure in which I was being entertained. Rounds of lusty snores indicated their oblivion of the hostess' impromptu festivity. After enduring the well meant kindness as long as the utmost limits of patience would sustain me, I excused myself, and returned to the hamlet and resorted to my hammock, with a deep sense of thankfulness and relief. The neighbors scattered to their homes. My hostess turned to her prayers before her household saint. In the gradually expiring light of a pine stick all soon became quiet, followed by darkness and sleep.

CHAPTER XX.

A NATIVE FARM—ONCE MORE ON THE ROAD—ARRIVAL AT SANTIAGO DE LOS CABALLEROS—SEÑOR JOSÉ M. GLAS—HOSPITALITY—THE CITY—A MASONIC CELEBRATION.

THE next morning I turned out at early dawn in hopes of getting started in time to reach the city before the heat of day. My hostess made her appearance in the rude doorway of the *bohio* in spectre attire, as if she had been very suddenly aroused. As I had an abundance of time, I set out on a tour of inspection about the premises. The rancho had an air of thrift about it which I had not yet seen in my journey. I attributed this fact to the superior intelligence, management, and industry of the late proprietor, who, as I have already stated, was an American negro. The house was one of the ordinary *palencas* in vogue among the middle class of the country. It was about fifteen feet in length and twelve or fourteen in depth, with two rooms, one on either side of a broad, open passage, running through from front to rear. The walls were made of a number of posts set perpendicularly in the the ground, so as to resemble a palisade. The word *palenca* means, properly, palisade. There were two rooms and the most primitive furniture. There were no windows. The door was without hinges or lock, and was lifted on and off like the shutters of a shop-window. Every variety of article in possession of the family was stowed away inside. A thatch roof covered the structure and extended about six feet beyond, on the front, so as to make a shelter for the occupants, and also answered excellently as a place to hang tobacco drying for the market. There is a style of *palenca* used by the better class of farmers, made by setting four upright posts in the ground. The walls are composed of rough lathing, split from small branches of trees and closely woven between the posts. A coat of plaster is then put on the lathing both inside and out. The structure is covered with a roof of palm thatching, arranged in a sort of pyramidal form.

 The farm consisted of about four acres, enclosed within a strong fence. The chief growth was tobacco, though a patch of corn had also been planted, and looked well.

My peon now notified me of his readiness to continue to the city. I bade farewell to my kind hostess, not overlooking a few American half-dollars as a tangible recognition of her hospitality. A few small pieces distributed amongst the youngsters that had crowded around to witness my departure also made a visible impression upon their minds.

I followed my peon, and my retinue followed me, back to the main road. After a brief journey, at eight o'clock, on the morning of June 27, 1869, Sunday, I entered the city of Santiago de los Caballeros before most of the inhabitants were up.

As hotels or lodging-houses are unknown conveniences in San Domingo, the traveler on the island is compelled to accept the hospitality of his friends, or, if a stranger, to make friends and mention his wants. I was fortified with a letter to Señor Don José M. Glas, a wealthy exporter of tobacco. I made my way under the direction of my peon to his residence. The gentleman himself was not out of bed, but his place was generously supplied at this juncture by Señor Rodriguez. I was requested to have my baggage taken down, and to make my quarters, during my stay, with Señor Glas. I settled with my peon, and gave men and boys of the motley crew, now formed in the street, a present of a small sum of money, greatly to their delight.

At noon my host made his appearance. He was a small, middle-aged man, with an exceedingly business like air. After exchanging a few preliminary courtesies, he invited me to breakfast. My rustic and frugal fare on the way had whetted my appetite to a keen edge. I now found considerable interest in demolishing a beefsteak, and a quota of bread and fried bananas, moistened in a liberal supply of fine claret.

After breakfast, at which Señor Rodriguez was also a guest, I was invited to the parlor up stairs. My room had already been assigned me, so I was not long in feeling quite at home. My host very soon excused himself, as the day had been set apart for the celebration of the Masonic festival of St. John. He informed me that he was the Master of the Lodge of Freemasons, Nuevo Monde, (Number 1,) and was compelled to superintend the proceedings of the day. On this subject the Señor and myself being of the same acquaintance, I was invited to join in the exercises. I agreed to do so in the evening.

My host's residence answered the three purposes

of a place for the sale of merchandise, a store-house for tobacco, and a residence. The latter was in the rear, facing on a paved court. The building was of stone and mortar, and was very commodious. Being alone, after resting during the heat of the day, I took a stroll about the city. I also particularly enjoyed the view from a small hill, not far off, which gave me an admirable idea of the situation and topography of the surrounding country.

Next to the capital, Santiago de los Caballeros is the chief city in San Domingo. The site is upon a swell in a plain stretching along the right bank of the Yaque river. The adjacent country is extremely fertile and beautiful. The city was built in the year 1504. It was laid out in squares, the streets running at right angles, and was surrounded by earthworks. In the endless civil commotions which inaugurated the present century in San Domingo, the city was repeatedly attacked and occupied, and finally was almost entirely destroyed. It was pillaged by the French during their contests with the Spaniards. In 1805, Dessaline having determined to possess the Spanish part of the island, commenced an invasion. This act of aggression was carried on in two columns. The Haytians were compelled to raise the siege of San Domingo in consequence of the appearance of a

French squadron. Dessalines was ferocious in his rage over this event. On Good Friday, 1805, the rear guard of Clervaux's retreating column, commanded by Christophe, occupied Santiago. Notwithstanding many fair promises, Christophe set fire to the churches and demolished the town. A number of the inhabitants, including six priests, were ruthlessly murdered.

Judging from the ruins, such as broken walls and shattered arches, isolated pillars, and other evidences of spacious buildings, the old Spanish city showed unmistakable signs of an inland seat of society and trade. To-day the rubbish and foundation walls are all that have survived the former activity and importance of Santiago de los Caballeros. The modern town, though well built, is less extensive in design and less extravagant in the dimensions of its buildings. But one church escaped the devastations of the invaders. The climate of the surrounding country, I was informed, is famous for its salubrity. The population of the city at the time of my visit was not less than three thousand souls. The district, governed by Señor Don Pacheco, contained a population of about fifteen thousand human beings.

In the early days the city was much larger than it is now. It was then the principal centre for the accommodation of the gold taken from the Cibao, and to be turned into coin or ingots. Santiago, in those palmy days, was literally a city of goldsmiths.

To-day, the chief trade of the city is the exportation of tobacco and the supply of the people of the district with such imported articles as they need. The planters from the surrounding country here bring their tobacco and dispose of it to the large purchasers or agents, who send it to the coast on pack-mules.

During my evening perambulations near the city I was shown what was considered an average tobacco plantation. I found it not more than six acres in area. The lot, for it appears like nothing more, was surrounded by a *palisar*, or staked fence, made by driving strong stakes and weaving cross-strips between them, securing the strips with the stems of a vine called *bahuca*. One plantation near the city was surrounded by a beautiful *maya* hedge. The *maya* is very generally used for this purpose. The plant is a long-leaved evergreen, with a thorny edge, and very hardy.

The mode of planting tobacco, from accounts, was decidedly primitive. It was merely necessary to scratch a hole and drop in a few seeds. In due time, with further scratching, so as to keep down the weeds, a fine healthy plant came up, and in a few months was ready for market. The comparatively large quantity of tobacco brought to Santiago gave rise to a lively trade between the city and the country, as well as the sea-coast. Business houses, therefore, were well stocked with goods of all kinds, principally of European manufacture. American goods were very scarce, mainly on account of the ruinous policy of our Government in regard to the commercial and business interest of the country.

After all I saw, I entertained in my mind no doubt whatever but that, under a permanent and secure government, Santiago and its tributary districts would become the centre of a large and wealthy population. The fertile soil, instead of yielding nourishment to a rank, and, in a commercial point of view profitless, vegetation would bring forth, in response to the industrious efforts of human toil, valuable crops of tobacco, coffee, cotton, sugar, and many other articles of export.

Night coming on, I returned to the residence of my host. I found dinner awaiting me. Apologizing for the delay, after partaking of his hospitable board, we set out together for the scene of the evening festivities. Entering a large room, a crowd of men and women, the fashion of the city and vicinity, were gathered, and about to begin at the dance. A band set up a great din, regardless of harmony or measure. I remained a spectator, contrary to repeated requests to join in. The men were all well dressed. The ladies, mostly mulattoes, were generally very tasteful in their toilettes, and added, in many cases, the charms of beauty of face and figure, and the grace of motion. At least three-fifths were of negro blood. Some of the Caucassian race were so dark that they might have been taken for negroes by descent. In San Domingo distinction of color, in social life, is entirely unknown, though a rivalry of race, black, mixed, and white, in politics and governmental affairs has led, in many cases, to trouble and violent contention.

At midnight, leaving the gay throng to their amusements, I withdrew, and returned to the house of my friend.

CHAPTER XXI.

CAONABO, CHIEF OF THE CIBAO.

PREVIOUS to the arrival of the Spaniards, Hayti was divided into five parts, each under the dominion of a great Cacique. Marien, under the friendly Cacique, Guacanagan, stretched along the northern coast, from the west, as far as the great river Yaque. The bitter Guarionex held sway in that beautiful region of the interior, known as the Royal Vega. Cotabanama, the Cacique of Higuey, exercised dominion in the east, his territories lying south of the Bay of Samana and Yuna river, and west of the Ozama. Behechio, the brother-in-law of Caonabo, ruled the people of Xaragua, remote from the country occupied by the Spaniards, extending along the southwestern side. Of all the native rulers of the country, however, the Carib chieftain, Caonabo, was the most implacable foe to the foreign intruders,

His principality, known in the tongue of the country as Maguana, occupied part of the southern coast, from the Ozama to the lakes, extending across the centre of the island, and included the wild and rugged country along the southern slopes of the Cibao. The administration of these territorial divisions was a rude type of the fuedal system. The grand Caciques held general sway over a number of tributary caciques, who accorded allegiance and performed military service with their retainers.

Both Columbus and his brother, Don Bartholomew, the Adelantado, who was left in command, had been much annoyed by the inveterate hostility of Caonabo. His fierce warriors often descended from their mountain strongholds and threw the country into the greatest consternation. Any luckless Castilian, or small detachment, or train of supplies, was in danger of being taken by the predatory subjects of this bold and daring chieftain.

The martial skill and resolution of Caonabo was well known to Columbus and to the Adelantado. Aroused at the licentiousness and violence of the Spanish soldiery in the Vega, he had congregated a vast army of an hundred thousand men. This immense army of native valor, under the feared Caonabo, made its appearance upon the plain and adjacent forests surrounding the fortress of St. Thomas. This interior stronghold, established by Columbus himself, during his first visit to the Cibao, stood upon the banks of the Yanique, eighteen leagues from Isabella, and upon the main road from that point through the Cibao and the Vega.* The daring Alonzo de Ojeda was in command, and was so closely pressed that even his reckless courage was put to severe straits before he was succored from his perilous situation.

To wage war upon this powerful Cacique, and that too in his mountain fastnesses, was a subject of no small concern. As we have seen, Caonabo had displayed his resources in point of numbers, and, even if his troops were scattered, the chief himself displayed remarkable fortitude. While Columbus was pondering over what he should do, Alonzo de Ojeda relieved him of his anxiety, by volunteering to take the mountain chieftain, and to deliver him alive. Coming from any one than Alonzo de Ojeda, Columbus would have rebuked the rash proffer as the gasconade of a braggart. Ojeda had already earned for himself the reputation of a resolute soldier. The record of his acts had already gone forth over the island, and his very name was a terror. In his

* The traces of the fort still exist near Yanique, on a farm called La Fortaleza. The place is now overgrown with trees.

reckless exploits he had, time and again, scoured the country, and had put to flight almost an hundred times his numbers. His fame was as great among his countrymen, as his feats of daring were terrible in the minds of the natives. It may well be imagined, then, that Columbus but too gladly received the bold words of Ojeda, and accepted his heroic services.

All was ready for the desperate undertaking. The gallant Ojeda had selected ten of the best and truest men he could find—men whose courage he had tried and knew how far it could be trusted. They were well armed with sword and lance. Their horses were clad in polished steel. With this small but indomitable retinue, Ojeda left the protecting walls of the garrison and boldly launched forth into the wild and rugged dominions of the terrible Caonabo, the mighty chieftain of the Cibao.

The audacity of Ojeda's movement struck Caonabo with surprise and admiration. He had penetrated sixty leagues within his territories, and now saluted him in his most populous town and capital. Surrounding the little band were thousands of trained warriors who, at the beck of Caonabo, would gladly have fallen upon the hated strangers and have torn them to pieces.

But Ojeda, undaunted, with an air of confidence and indifference, completely disarmed the chieftain. They were at once on the best of friendly terms. The two exchanged greetings and Ojeda accepted the hospitality of the chieftain. Ojeda persuaded Caonabo that his visit was of a peaceable character, and that he had brought some valuable presents from Guamiquina, the chief of all the Spaniards. This act of condescension had a good effect.

Ojeda now tried the next step. By means of the insinuating arts of laudation and mild argument, the chieftain was urged to repair to Isabella, and there to make a lasting treaty with the Spaniards, so that all ill feeling between them, and the subjects of the chief, might be amicably arranged, and to last for all time. It is said that Ojeda offered the bell in the church at Isabella, as the reward of this great act of friendship. The natives had a great reverence for this simple piece of mechanism. They imbued it with supernatural powers. Its deep tones, falling on the quiet air of the surrounding forests, were construed into a language which the Spaniards understood; and as Caonabo himself prowled about these same forests within hearing of the mysterious sounds, he paused upon some convenient height, and was struck with amazement when he saw the

Spaniards respond by hastening, from all directions, towards the little church.

The offer could not be resisted. Caonabo agreed to go with Alonzo de Ojeda, and obtain the wonderful being, which, as he thought, came from Turey, the skies. All was ready, but Ojeda discovered a vast array of native warriors marshaled, awaiting the chieftain.

At this warlike array Ojeda was annoyed. But assuming an air of indifference, he interrogated Caonabo as to the intent of all that martial display. The proud chieftain, deigning to reply, said it did not become one so great to visit strangers unattended. Ojeda was nonplussed at the formidable turn-out. He feared to permit so strong a force to draw near to the town. He feared treachery. With the readiness of one accustomed to meeting obstacles, he conceived an ingenious means of taking the chieftain captive. Appearing indifferent to the pageantry and numbers around him, Ojeda, and his handful of men, moved by the side of Caonabo. The vast retinue wound down mountain heights, through dark defiles, or stretched out upon the plain. Ojeda was animated. By his vivacity of manner he strove to disarm suspicion. In this he admirably succeeded. Halting upon the verdant banks of one of the larger tributaries of the Neyba, Ojeda displayed a pair of manacles, highly wrought and polished, so that they looked like silver. Caonabo was delighted. With a mixture of humor while extolling the value of the intended gift, Ojeda said that they were used by his sovereigns in solemn dances. The chieftain was flattered by the proffer. Ojeda now, with consummate subtlety, proposed to Caonabo that he go with him to the river and bathe. He should then be decorated with the royal gift, and be mounted on his horse, and return among his brave warriors in all the state and ceremony of a Castilian monarch.

Allurements of so invincible a nature, gratifying equally his cupidity and his pride, could not be resisted. Ojeda and the chieftain descended to the stream. Caonabo bathed in its waters, and was after aided upon a horse behind Ojeda. The manacles were now put on, under the admiring eyes of the chief himself. Now came the decisive, desperate moment, the crisis which would find the formidable Caonabo a captive, an unwilling but powerless fugitive from his people, or Alonzo de Ojedo would find himself, at so untimely a moment, cut short in a career of world-wide renown.

Ojeda drove the rowels deep into his horse's side. The high-mettled animal bounded forward. Ojeda, followed by his handful of heroes, described a circle in the open space. The admiring warriors of Caonabo gave way to the fearless Spaniards. The circle grew larger by degrees. Finally, making one vast range of the surrounding space, Ojeda and his followers, with the astounded Caonabo, disappeared in the adjacent forest. In the gloom of overhanging branches, and protected from the vision of his warriors by the intervening undergrowth, the Spaniards drew close to the bewildered chieftain. Swords were drawn. In a moment the life of Caonabo was threatened as the forfeit of the least alarm. The great chief of the Cibao submissively yielded to imperious fate. He was quickly bound hands and feet. Ojeda, beckoning to his followers, dashed into the stream.

Leaving this river between Caonabo and his warriors, the daring little band dashed rapidly for the coast. Over sixty leagues of mountain and forest lay between them and Isabella. Undaunted they shot forward into this dangerous space. Populous towns lined the route. Timidly they approached, but reaching their confines fearlessly, dashed through them with shouts and brandishing of glistening steel. The terrified natives fled into their houses. Ojeda and his regal prize went repeating this act of reckless daring, and spreading consternation everywhere along his route.

Imagine, then, the delight of Columbus when he saw the gallant Alonzo, de Ojeda, with his ten trusty cavaliers, bearing within the protecting walls of Isabella the feared monarch of the Cibao.

Caonabo, when brought in the presence of Columbus, drew himself up with all that wild independence that had often caused his subjects to tremble. He looked with haughty disdain upon the Admiral. He adverted to his fearful vengeance upon the infant settlement at Vavidad. He even told how he designed, at an early day, to assail Columbus and his detested followers in the very walls he was then a captive. He was as bold as if still surrounded with all the power and importance of regal sway.

It is one of the bright pages in Columbus's fame that he gave orders that Caonabo should be treated with kindness and consideration. He even accorded to him part of his own residence, but, determined that so formidable an enemy should not slip him, he loaded him with chaims. The conduct of Caonabo under these unhappy circumstances showed his loftiness of soul, his elevation of character, his exaltation of moral and physical courage. Towards Columbus the unfortunate chieftain preserved his haughty bearing throughout. When the Admiral entered the prison apartments all rose out of homage to his rank and services. Caonabo did not even condescend to notice him; but towards Alonzo de Ojeda he felt the deepest respect and admiration. He appreciated even the daring which had brought him to his abject condition in the hands of the detested strangers. When Ojeda entered, Coanabo rose and exhibited the profoundest signs of recognition and respect. In response to a question as to why he showed this preference towards one who had been the direct cause of all his misfortunes, the chief replied that Guamiquina (Columbus) would not have dared to penetrate his dominions, much less to seize him among his own warriors; that to Ojeda belonged that honor, and he did him reverence for an act which none but one so brave would have dared to undertake.

The unfortunate Caonabo was sent to Spain. Never more did he view the wild grandeur of his native mountains. Never more did he lead his fierce warriors to battle against the hated invaders. His downfall was the death knell of his race.

Seven thousand (some authorities say as high as a hundred thousand) warriors, under Manicaotex, the brother to the fallen Cacique, inspired by the beautiful Anacaona, the wife of Caonabo, assembled to avenge his loss. They invested the fortress of St. Thomas. Here Ojeda was once more in command. Ojeda, strengthened in numbers, fell upon the advancing battalions of natives. Unable to resist this fearless onslaught, Manicaotex soon found his army crumble away from under him. His own life paid the penalty of the conflict. His vaunted and avenging army was now nothing more than a fugitive route.

Thus ends the story of Caonabo, the monarch of the Cibao. With his downfall begins that chapter of unparalleled woe inflicted upon an inferior race by implacable, avaricious, and relentless conquerors.

CHAPTER XXII.

THE PERPLEXITIES OF TRAVEL—AN UNTIMELY JOLLI-
FICATION—A NOCTURNAL INTERRUPTION—
TWO UNPROTECTED FEMALES.

HAVING made up my mind in the beginning that unnecessary delay would be but a waste of time, the morning after my arrival at Santiago de los Caballeros, I completed negotiations in view of my departure the same afternoon. Shortly after my arrival I arranged for the use of three horses, to convey me and my baggage and supplies to the capital. A peon was to be furnished with the horses. I also employed a servant. The hour of my start was fixed at two o'clock in the afternoon. The preparations for the journey I left to my servant, with instructions to have everything in readiness to set out at the hour named. During the morning I called to present my respects to the Governor of the district, and at the same time to have my passport countersigned and to take leave. The Governor was extremely courteous, and having presented me to the partner of his official honors and domestic responsibilities, produced several bottles of ale as a voucher of hospitality. The Governor's wife was extremely robust in person, but lively nevertheless, and only suspended her activity in the performance of her household duties, to give me a look of recognition and a clean glass.

Having returned to my friend's house, about the time that my horses were to be on hand, I found no signs of either the quadrupeds or the bipeds. An hour over the time had passed, and still no prospects. To cap the climax, my indefatigable Jacques had lost his customary serenity in divers potations of *aquardienta*. I despatched a straggling mercenary to hurry up the horses, gave Jacques a lecture on the value of temperance in hours of business, and withdrew to nap off the choler that had already disturbed the harmony of my departure.

It was late in the afternoon before the horses made their appearance. I now enjoyed, on my part, a provoking diversion in setting out on a reconnoitering expedition through the town in search of my servant. I found him, in delightful and oblivious repose, under the full beam of the afternoon sun. Judging from appearances, he had withdrawn for recuperation some time before, when the sun was much higher in the firmament. The tropical luminary had changed position, but Señor Jacques, failing to make a corresponding movement, was fairly broiling. A few cuffs and a liberal administration of my cane brought him to his senses. His mental lucidity was no better than his locomotion; both were seriously tangled. Under the circumstances, I considered calmnesss the best policy, and however much, at intervals, I experienced a disposition to flourish my cane about his woolly *cranium*, he experienced no such deserved commendation of his conduct. There was one argument by way of palliation, and that was, the supplies and baggage, I discovered, were all ready and packed in the palm woven panniers, to be put upon the horses. It was necessary to get out of the reach of further libations.

After several charitable and alternate applications of boot-leather and cane upon the sweltering carcass of my vagabond servant, by way of a final demonstration, I shook hands with a number of citizens who had assembled to see me off. I could not sufficiently express my grateful feelings in return for their generous hospitality and repeated kindness. I quickly mounted my horse, and once more waving farewell, set out on the long journey of fifty leagues—one hundred and fifty miles.

I had determined to pay no more attention to my servant. By this time he was in that self-satisfied condition, very forcibly illustrated when he spread himself with his back against my friend's house, and stood there grinning and giving vent to a variety of incomprehensible observations and maudlin criticism. My friends could not resist the impulse to enjoy the scene. As I rode off, followed by the peon, also mounted and leading the extra horse, the vagabond, against the wall, suddenly recovered from his relaxation, and sobered up sufficiently to promise to mount.

The scene, at this stage of my exit from the inland emporium of San Domingo, was extremely ludicrous. The equestrian performances of the supple but unsteady Jacques were marvelous. His ideas of accuracy in applying his forces, in jumping on the horse, were sadly at fault. He made an admirable spring, but lit upon his stomach; and, in his efforts to right himself, made a few very violent kicks in the rear, after which he managed to work himself in a vertical position, with his head down, along the other side of the horse, while his heels were spasmodically performing in the air. This complicated movement was finished by rolling off, on the other side, and measuring his length on the ground.

After the completion of this fruitless attempt, I required my peon to haul the vagabond out of the dirt and to assist him in the saddle. This being done, I once more got started, the peon leading the way and the servant bringing up the rear, in a manner reflecting very little credit upon his horsemanship.

I directed the peon to take the main road for La Vega. After a short ride along the bluffy banks of the Yaque, crossing a small tributary, in which were a number of watermen with their donkeys, our route left the main stream. The road was hard and much traveled. A number of natives, carrying their goods on their heads, or, more conveniently, on the backs of donkeys and bullocks, were passing towards, or arriving from, the city. My servant, for the rest of the day's journey, was the most edifying as well as obnoxious person I had to encounter. His volubility prompted him to accost every person on the way, and in this manner made, not only himself, but me, very conspicuous. Before I was a mile out of the city, he had captured an aged priest, mounted on a donkey, and, with drunken dignity, introduced him:

I found the priest a very agreeable traveling companion, full of information, and regretted that he was not going the whole distance. After continuing several miles on my way, he left by a cross-road to return to the city.

While I was engaged with the priest, having, in the beginning, silenced the tireless tongue of Jacques, it seemed the vagabond had scraped the acquaintance of another traveler. Hardly had the priest turned off the road, than this newly made friend was presented. The stranger informed me that he was a general, and belonged to the Dominican army. He also gave his name, but his tongue was not in any condition for very lucid vocalization, so that I did not understand. I was deeply impressed with his martial rank, particularly as he communicated the fact every few minutes, with an impressive drawing of his chin upon his bosom, a friendly and admiring stroke of the abdominal regions for his breast, and usually wound up with a suggestive hiccough. The general insisted upon my passing the night at his house. He was seconded in his proposition by the intolerable Jacques, who probably anticipated that the vibratory motion of his friend's spinal column was suggestive of better cheer than he would be likely to have at a road-side hamlet.

It required no small amount of diplomacy to extricate myself from the determined importunities of my maudlin companion. I positively refused, a number of times, when he invariably reminded me that he was a general. When I saw him whooping and yelling and spurring down a road, diverging from the main one, I informed Mr. Jacques that I had no desire to cultivate any more such acquaintances.

As the distance from the city increased, the number of people on the road diminished, and so did Jacques' enthusiasm in proportion. I now gave some instructions, which I wished to be observed on the journey. The peon, with the baggage, was to ride always in advance, about fifty yards. I put myself in the centre, and required my servant to follow close in the rear, so as to be conveniently at hand. The peon was an old man, over sixty years of of age, very quiet, and wore an expression of deplorable mental darkness. He had on a native *sombrero* of plaited palm leaf, a check shirt, and dirty white cotton pantaloons. Strapped to his waist was a ponderous *machete*, or sword, which looked as if it might have been handed down from the days of Nimrod. Jacques was arrayed in a suit of threadbare broadcloth, evidently borrowed for the occasion. He formerly, that is when he left the city, two hours before, wore a straw hat. In his ribald performances he had severed the relations between the crown and the rim. The crown was now well pulled over his ears, the rim had dropped down about his neck, and served as a rude collar of the Elizabeth age. He also wore a *machete*, but of less formidable proportions than that of the peon. This same individual was about thirty years of age, and sported a decidedly idiotic face. He had been a sailor, and had seen enough of the world to acquire all the deviltry he had the capacity to learn.

About six miles from the city, night coming on very rapidly, I despatched Jacques, who was henceforth to comprise the two functions of servant and aid-de-camp, ahead to look for accommodations for the night. The exertions of the afternoon had evidently much exhausted him, so that the nearest *bohio* was selected. Without objection on the part of the occupants we rode into the enclosure. I dismounted, and saw that the animals, upon which so much depends in a journey like the present, were at once relieved of their packs, and turned out to pasture. I now entered the *bohio*, and was very promptly and pompously presented to the superannuated pair who were the denizens of the establishment. Everything wore the most poverty-stricken appearance. The old man, in a state of semi-nudity, was lying upon a rude bench in the open passage. The aged female, his wife, was making preparations to retire. The cabin was built of upright posts, very rudely and irregularly driven in the ground. The bare earth constituted the floor.

As it was raining, I had a bullock skin, used in covering the packs, spread upon the ground-floor inside, in the open passage. On this, after a light supper, with my saddle and hammock for a pillow, I threw myself down to rest. I had been asleep but a short time when I was aroused by a strange sensation. I reached out, and in doing so took hold of the horn of an animal. Upon further investigation I found the cause of the interruption was a goat pasturing upon my beard.

This first episode in my slumbers was followed very soon after by the arrival of two young women with a donkey. The animal was driven into the passage-way, where the pack was removed. The women, after disposing of the donkey, and removing a portion of their very limited attire, bestirred themselves about a fire in the open air, in the rear of the hut, preparing a repast of baked plantains. While these were cooking, the women by the fire bathed in a large calabash. I have never found any very inconvenient modesty among the country people of the tropics anywhere, but this was decidedly the most indifferent exhibition of two chestnut-colored forms of artistic symmetry. After they had finished their ablutions, the women mumbled over their rosary, ate their plantains, and turned into rest, occupying the same limited space with myself, regardless of my presence.

CHAPTER XXIII.

CHARMING SCENERY—LA VEGA REAL—THE TOWN OF LA VEGA—HOSPITALITIES.

AFTER this night of adventure, and particularly being obliged to turn out every now and then to shake the fleas out of my habiliments, I felt no reluctance in making an early start. My watch, greatly to my inconvenience, had fallen out of repair. The moon was shining brightly, but I could observe no indications of approaching dawn. After several astronomical observations, alternating with a renewal of my labors among the fleas, I came to the conclusion to start. I aroused my people, and hastened them in getting their morning bite, and saddling and packing the animals.

Having paid the old man for his hospitality, I got upon the road, and before the heat of the day, had made a fair journey. The road wound through a charming country. It had descended, from the giddy summits of the northern range, into a low and open section, covered with innumerable small valleys, hills, and crystal streams, and then again ascended, crossing smaller hills. The diversity of landscape and variety of vegetation was enchanting beyond description. Small savannas and beautiful groves opened in constant succession, and took the place of the dark forests of mahogany and *campeche*, which covered the mountain regions. The *almendra*, or wild almond, the mango, with its dense foliage of perenial green, the satin tree, the glossy foliage of the guanabana, the wild orange, the plantain, the pale green groves of bananas, the cocoa-nut, the towering palm, with its great overhanging leaves, the luxuriant foliage of the pomegranate, the deep green of the coffee tree, the lime tree, with its ripening fruit, all blended in endless change of color and form, with the humbler unknown and uncared for varieties.

The road crossed the limpid, swift-running waters of the Verde, so named by Columbus on his visit to the interior over three centuries before. The stream was evidently quite formidable during seasons of heavy rains. At the time I crossed it, it was not more than eighteen inches in depth.

The most striking feature in the ever-changing landscape during the journey was El Pinal, or Pine Mountain, along the base of which ran the narrow road-path. The mountain was covered, from foot to summit, with dense and extensive forests of pine, while the adjoining hills were clothed with a vegetation which seemed as if it belonged to another sphere. This peculiar freak of nature was most remarkable, as the pine was confined solely to this one spot, while all the rest of the vegetation was tropical. The wood of these forests is used by the country people in the place of candles. It is a sort of pitch pine, and is cut in long thin sticks; one end is ignited, and the stick is laid down horizontally, in which position it consumes slowly, and distributes a subdued, yellowish, red light.

Reaching the charming heights of Santo Cerro I halted for rest and to graze the animals. Meanwhile the now sobered Jacques produced the *macutas* containing the supplies. Beneath the grateful shade of a grove of mangoes and lime trees I ate a hearty breakfast, which he had laid out for me upon a spread, made of the dried skin of the young growth of the palm tree.

From the summit of Santo Cerro, Columbus, during his first visit to the interior, feasted his eyes upon the blooming and voluptuous bosom of nature, which lay opened before him. He now beheld a prospect which exceeded even the matchless beauties of the regions which he had already traversed. Sweeping savannas, groves and meandering streams, suddenly burst into view. In the enthusiasm of the moment, Columbus named this beautiful region La Vega Real, the Royal Meadow. And still further, with that reverent and thankful spirit which pervaded all the great achievements in his career of discovery, Columbus made a rude cross, and planted it in full view of this crowning handiwork of the Creator of the Universe, A chapel was subsequently built upon the spot occupied by the cross, and here the people came to lay floral tributes to the memory of the great "Colon." The cross, after standing for some years, was removed to the cathedral, in San Domingo city, and may be seen by the traveler in one of the side chapels in that immense and ancient edifice. The cross is said to have been the first planted on the island.

After passing an hour in this delightful spot I mounted my horse, spread that indispensable companion, my umbrella, and once more set forth under the burning sun. The road now made a rapid descent of the mountain, passing near the ruins of the ancient city of La Conception de la Vega, which was destroyed, by an earthquake, in 1564. The road now crossed the Camou, a deep and rapid stream. A short distance beyond I reached the modern city of La Vega. The distance from Santiago de los Caballeros to La Vega is fifteen leagues. The road nowhere is more than a mere opening cut through the forests. In some places it is wide—in others narrow and impassable, except for animals. It would be impossible to make the journey in any sort of wheeled vehicle.

On entering the town I proceeded immediately to the Plaza, facing which were the headquarters of the Governor of the Province. A squad of eight semi-nude soldiers were lounging about the dilapidated building. I dismounted and entered. The Governor General, Roman Guyman, was was not in, but having sent a soldier out in search of him, he soon appeared. After a few words of civility, by way of preliminary, I handed over my passport, which he signed.

Having with me a letter of introduction to one of the leading citizens of the place, General Enrique Galacia, I set out in search of that gentleman. I found him confined to his bed, and quite ill. He received me, however, and apologized not only for his condition, but his inability to show me some courtesy. He invited me to pass the night at his house, a kind proposition, I apologetically declined, as I hoped to still make a good journey before swinging my hammock.

After a short conversation I thanked the General for his proffered hospitality and withdrew. As I was leaving, he said that he regretted he was unable to accompany me a few miles on my journey.

La Vega is situated on an eminence overlooking the Camou. It has a very squalid appearance, and is the seat of a community of not more than one thousand souls. La Vega was founded in 1564, immediately after the destruction of the old town of La Vega de la Conception by an earthquake. The present place owes its dilapidated condition to the devastating hand of the Haytian soldiers, under Christophe, who very nearly destroyed it in 1805. It is the seat of government for the province of La Vega. The town possesses a few stores and a large cathedral. The population of the province is small. The people live by raising a little tobacco, which they transport to the market at Santiago on pack animals. On a small stream, a short distance beyond the town, I halted for several hours to allow the sun to make a considerable distance in its downward course in the heavens. While the mindful Jacques was renewing his foraging expedition into the *macutas*, I retired to a shady spot and indulged in a refreshing bath in the limpid waters that coursed over a beautiful pebbly bed at my feet.

CHAPTER XXIV.

CROSSING LA VEGA REAL—UNPARALLELED BEAUTY OF LANDSCAPE—GRAZING HERDS—CROSSING THE YUNA—COTUY—CAMP IN THE MOUNTAINS.

T was fully three o'clock in the afternoon before I again ventured in the heat of the sun. The road now debouched upon a low, open, and well-drained country, consisting of broad savannas and beautiful groves. In the dim distance, on all sides, rose the blue hazy masses of the mountain ranges, their loftier summits enveloped in driving clouds. It was this region of unparalleled beauty and fertility, upon which Columbus gazed with such enthusiastic admiration after leaving the circumscribed scenery of the mountains. The savannas resembled the finest prairies of Illinois, with the additional feature of being covered, year in and year out, with a carpet

of luxuriant and perennial green. There was also a fragrance of groves which broke the monotony of an expansive champagne country.

During the rest of the day's journey I found, grazing upon these savannas, herds of the sleekest, fattest cattle I had ever seen. These herds, descended from the original stock, imported by the Spaniards, prospered remarkably upon the abundant pastures and pure waters of La Vega Real. It was from here that the island derived its beef, which was to be purchased readily at from six to eight dollars a head on the ground, and from three to five cents per pound, net, in the town. The cattle ran wild, and increased in numbers without any attention whatever, or at least very little, from man.

The sacrifice and waste of cattle which had occurred in late years, through the incursions of revolutionary parties, gave rise, not long before my visit, to a proclamation from the Government, prohibiting exportation. Previously, there was a large trade in cattle for the seaports, to be shipped to the neighboring islands. Under the ordinary circumstances of increase and consumption, I should judge, from what I saw, the supply of beef was amply sufficient to answer the needs of the entire population of the island. I was most surprised to find a section, teeming with fertility, and abounding in cattle, almost entirely without any signs of human habitation. During the afternoon I did not meet a single person on the road, and saw but two small *hattoos* occupied by herders, to remind me that the country was more than a beautiful, uninhabited wild.

An afternoon rain may be considered a sure thing every day during the season in San Domingo. To rain in the morning is very rare. It was after a practical experience in the former meteorological fact that I arrived, soon after sunset, in a very comfortless condition, at a rude *bohio*, a short distance off the road. Jacques, as usual, had preceded my arrival, and made satisfactory arrangements for a night's shelter.

By a very material miscalculation of time, the next morning I got started inconveniently early, and had at least a three hour's ride by moonlight before dawn. In this uncertain alternation of dim light and embarrassing shadow, in passing across savannas and through groves, progress was only made against a diversity of inconveniences, not the least of which was the crossing of several small streams.

The road between Santiago and Le Vega, though impassable for vehicles, was broad enough to have made a regular highway of travel and traffic, and only needed the removal of obstructions, here and there, and the grading of the slopes of the hills. Between Le Vega and Cotuy the paths, in places in the lower lands, were worn into deep tranverse furrows and holes. My horse took several occasions to stumble over the intervening little ridges of earth, and before escaping this difficult place, had me well besmeared and splashed with mud. I had now reached a section that had evidently experienced very heavy rains. The great meadows, which I was informed were hard and dry during other seasons, were now soggy and difficult to cross. To make haste slowly, I found was by all means the safer course. The rivers were high and difficult to pass. Neither were there any canoes, nor boats, for the convenience of travel; and such a structure as a bridge was not known on the whole Dominican portion of the island.

Quite early in the morning, judging by instinct, for, as I have already stated, my time-piece was not in a going humor, I struck the bank of the beautiful Yuna, and pursued it for some distance to the ford. From the width of the stream, and the rapidity of its current, it was apparent that heavy rains had fallen upon its head-waters. Here was a quandary—no bridge, no boat. As for myself it was an easy matter to get over, and then would not have been the first time I had swam a river, leading my horse. But I was very effectually disconcerted in regard to my baggage and provisions. I was entirely ignorant of the depth of the turbid flood, and so were my servant and peon.

To cross was a necessity, no matter what the consequences, particularly if only the loss of food and a small supply of clothing. My retinue traveled very light in the latter articles, carrying all their effects on their backs.

I decided to test the depth of the stream by wading. Jacques, a blatant rogue on dry land, rebelled against risking the dangers of the stream. I was about to make the venture myself, when a native appeared out of the brush, on the opposite bank. Jacques, relieved of his anxiety, practised his vocal powers by negotiating with the native across the stream. Under promise of the liberal compensation of a dollar the sable son of San Domingo removed his apparel, which consisted of a pair of cotton pantaloons, and started in. The river was at least a hundred yards wide, and reached breast high in most places. The current was strong and rapid. I must confess I had my doubts about getting the contents of the panniers over without a soaking. But the crossing had to be made, and, therefore, the sooner accomplished the better.

The horses were unsaddled, and everything not transportable, the first trip, was left with the peon on the bank. In the elaborate costume of a felt hat I mounted my horse, Jacques imitating my example. My clothes were put in the panniers, which my biped transport now tied together and took on his head.

The native started into the water, followed by myself, while Jacques formed the rear guard. The force of the current required no little display of dexterous horsemanship. My animal seemed to lack instinct in the matter of crossing streams, and several times was about to give way to the current, when I was only enabled to hold him to his work by heading him obliquely up stream.

At last we reached the shallow water on the opposite shore, and dragged out upon the bank in good order.

While the native was on his way to bring over the peon, and the second set of panniers, I enjoyed an invigorating bath in the waters of the Yuna. After a comparatively short delay I found myself and party climbing a low bluff, upon which was situated the town of Cotuy. It was eight o'clock when I reached the headquarters of the *commandante* of the detachment of troops stationed there.

Cotuy is a provincial town of little or no importance. It is situated on the right bank of the Yuna. The surrounding country is very beautiful. The town, when I passed through it, had a population of not more than four or five hundred souls. It was founded in 1505, but never rose to any great importance, notwithstanding the fact that it was in a mining region, and near mines said to have been worked until 1747. The remains of a copper mine in the mountain of Maymon are still visible, not far off. Emeralds have been found, also iron ore of great purity exists in large quantities. It was also near the golden regions of the Cibao. Mackenzie says, in his narrative written about a quarter of a century ago, that 240,000 crowns of gold were struck off, in a single year, in the mint of Conception de la Vega from gold brought from this region.

With population and enterprise, and with more convenient means of access, Cotuy would, undoubtedly, become the centre of a large business. The rearing of cattle is now the chief industry of that region. In the mountain near at hand is the famous valley of Constance, where wheat is raised, and frequently the temperature becomes very cold.

I halted but a few moments in hunting up the commanding-general of the province, and, having my passport countersigned, pushed ahead for a secluded and cool spot by some rippling stream, where the animals could rest, and I could follow up my early morning's bite with something more substantial.

For a short distance beyond Cotuy, the savanna country continued, and then began to disappear in low hills and frequent valleys and streams. When the sun was still high, I passed a *hatto* by the way. Jacques, who evidently did not carry a very brave heart, suggested that this was the last habitation until after crossing the southern mountain range. The individual displayed almost open revolt when I informed him that we would sleep in the mountains that night. The old peon, who was a very docile creature, led off, under my directions, but with visible reluctance. The information given by the peon, led me to suppose that the range could be crossed by the practice of a little expeditious travel. The sun was still sufficiently high for a long journey, but that mattered little, as the prospect of so long a halt, the guest of a native establishment, was anything but inviting to me. A sleep in the mountains was luxury compared with that.

As I was leaving this village, several fierce looking cavaliers, with immense *sombreros*, huge spurs, and ponderous *machetes*, dashed back and forth along the road. As they passed, they saluted quite gallantly. Their peculiar actions, and particularly their enthusiastic and demonstrative equestrian performances, surprised me not a little. My cavalcade at this time huddled up in a very small space by rallying on me for moral support, to say the least. Nor could I learn the cause of these peculiar performances. The horsemen, galloping and yelling about, were a fierce looking set, and certainly I had no inclination to cultivate an acquaintance. I had my weapons put away; for the use or display of such opposition would be worse, a thousand times, than boldness united with courtesy. I was much relieved upon reaching the first mountain range to find that the gay and gorgeous cavaliers had disappeared.

My attempt to cross the mountains was fruitless. At sun-set, having crossed four ranges, I was informed that there were two more, higher than those behind, still beyond. The perilous heights, difficult ascents and descents, rendered it impracticable to travel with any degree of safety, except by day-light. The animals, also, had had a long and trying journey, and needed rest. Reaching a secluded spot in a deep gorge between two of the highest ranges in the mountains, I ordered a halt. A beautiful opening in the forest afforded sufficient pasturage. A mountain stream, pouring down from towering heights its limped contribution to the great watercourses, ran near by. My attendants did not relish their accommodations, but, by the use of a little emphatic language, the horses were unsaddled and picketed out, my hammock was swung between two trees, a fire was built, and supper was soon ready. As I paid no attention to their complaints, the two worthies speedily, and without further observation, looked out for their own comfort. Having given positive orders to be ready early in the morning, I threw myself in my hammock to catch a little rest.

CHAPTER XXV.

AN UMBRELLA AS AN EXPEDIENT IN A STORM—A TROPICAL SUNRISE—A FORAGING EXPEDITION—CROSSING THE OZAMA—LESSONS IN NATATION—THE ISABELLA—A NOVEL MODE OF FERRYING—ARRIVAL AT THE CITY GATE AFTER HOURS.

ALTHOUGH, in many respects, a bivouac in the forests of San Domingo is preferable to the protecting thatch-covered huts of the natives, still this also has its inconveniences. Swinging in a hammock, between two giant mahogany trees, is, unquestionably, an independent and convenient method of camping out. A hammock is always suggestive of listlessness or reverie. Swinging under the shade of trees away from the sweltering heat, it is a powerful temptation to indolence and oblivity of care. In my own case, however, at present, I did not find it so inviting. The night was excessively dark. Immense fire-bugs, or rather-beetles, were crawling or awkwardly flying about among the trees. The heavens were starless. Before retiring, I had received repeated annoying indications of the existence of that universal though diminutive tormentor, the mosquito. My foreign blood seemed to be marked out as the special object of their industrious and musical efforts. My demonstrations having attracted the inventive Jacques, that sable individual made a small fire close to my hammock. The smoke soon compelled my troublesome camp companions to seek other victims. While the smoke lasted I found a spell of refreshing sleep, but before the night was over encountered another disturbing cause. When I awoke it was raining quite heavily. As I was without a tent, or even a tent fly, I abandoned the hammock. My umbrella was the only shelter I had. Opening this, I seated myself at the foot of a tree and passed the rest of the night in practical meteorological reflections, and no little impatience, regarding the dilatory progress of the earth's revolution.

At length, worn out with waiting upon the first indications of approaching dawn, I had my two attendants making preparations for an immediate resumption of the journey. The discomforts and disturbances that I had experienced found no consideration with these productions of the soil, for both might have been heard the live-long night lustily snoring down all rain and mosquitoes.

I made the ascent of the first mountain, and had reached its summit by sunrise. As this was not a premeditated thing, the surprise was all the more appreciated. In the fresh air of the morning the view was enchanting. Crystal dew-drops sparkled upon the variegated foliage. The landscape possessed all that diversity and charm which always strikes the traveler with so much admiration in crossing the great mountains and broad savannas of the interior of San Domingo. Halting but a moment to catch a glimpse of the beautiful scene, I descended into the valley. Ascending the last range, the road-path followed the crest of a bold and giddy scarp. This was the last of the mountain heights to be surmounted. The view was now grand and extensive beyond all description. The country swept away in a series of broad savannas terminating in the distant hazy ocean. On the right lay the high peaks of Marianna Chica, Seven Points, and St. Martin's, defining the golden valley of the Rio Jaina (Hayna.) On the left the mountains diminished into a series of low hills, covered with alternating patches of trees and savannas.

The descent from this mountain was difficult and dangerous. Steep descents, high rocks, overgrowing trees and tangled undergrowth, combined with the rain to make this part of the journey anything but pleasant. At one point, my equestrianism was sadly tested, by my horse stumbling, while making a small descent in the broken and irregular side of the mountain. I managed to rein him up, sufficiently, in his stumbling and headlong descent, when, no longer able to recover himself, he fell upon his knees and rolled the rest of the way, while I discovered myself deposited in a clump of bushes.

Before reaching the savanna country the road passed through El Paso de la Veuda, or the Widow's Pass, so named, I was informed, in consequence of a fatal accident to a lady of wealth who, while traveling over the mountain, fell, with her horse, from one of the precipitous heights on this part of the road.

At the first suitable place, at the base of the mountain, I halted for breakfast, and to lay in a small supply of provisions for the rest of the journey. I despatched Jacques on a foraging expedition. After a brief absence he returned with no very encouraging evidences of the abundance of the country.

He had three hen's eggs, for which he paid an exorbitant price. A dozen bananas, and four immense discs of cassava bread, not less than two feet in diameter and about an eighth of an inch in thickness were the results of this foray. I had two of the eggs boiled, and ate them, to be certain of no accidents. A few moments after Jacques was industriously removing the wreck of the other egg from his pantaloons pocket. The bananas were delicious, but as the staff of life, cassava bread, bore too close a resemblance to saw-dust to induce me to lean much upon that.

This little incident of scarcity in a land of unexampled fertility, and possessing all the requirements of boundless agricultural wealth, was a fit commentary upon the extreme poverty, ruin, and neglect now prevailing on the island. The very soil and the forests, the vallies and to the highest peaks of the mountains, teem everywhere with such resources, that the mind fails to expand itself to comprehend their extent; and yet a single traveler found it difficult to procure a breakfast for himself and two attendants.

At very nearly noon I reached the *halto* San Pedro. This was a village of about a dozen houses. I passed it by without a halt. The country now was a succession of savannas, well drained and stretching off to the Ozama. The guide, probably not relishing another night in the open air, lead the advance more rapidly than usual. Upon being interrogated, he replied that he desired to get beyond the Isabella before dark. As I had no objection to that, we increased our velocity to a periodical trot.

I now began to find traces of the presence of a centre of trade, in this case, the capital. During the day I passed a number of pack-parties, either going to the city or returning to their homes. Sugar and tobacco were the staple articles being thus transported.

Owing to the rains, the guide led me off the main road to a side path, which tended to a crossing of the Ozama higher up. Reaching the stream, and looking into its rushing waters, I anticipated more of a task than I had experienced on the Yuna. I was, however, soon relieved of my anxiety by the peon taking my valise in front of him, and plunging in, without hesitation. I halted for a moment to witness the result, for I confidently expected to see a very speedy dissolution of horse, peon, and my valise, each taking its own course to the broad ocean, down the rushing waters of the Ozama. My superannuated attendant made the other side without accident, though the water was considerably more than belly deep on his horse. Not to be outdone, I started after. My horse showed some signs of rebellion, but after several plunges, subjecting me to an admirable shower-bath, sobered down to the work, and made the other side in good order. I carried out of the stream a pair of feet and legs soaking wet, as a reminder. Jacques came next, presenting a most comical and ape-like figure. With his hands he held firmly to the pummel of his straw saddle. His horse, not kept in the crossing, first promenaded directly up stream. The indignant Jacques let go with one hand long enough to give his quadruped an emphatic jerk. The horse, taking the hint, made a very expeditious movement down stream. Jacques set up a well-accented soliloquy in bad Spanish. Before proceeding far on the downward course, it seemed as if the bottom had fallen out of the stream, for very suddenly the horse went down to his ears, and Señor Jacques found himself sandwiched between the two panniers, which being almost empty, began to float. The vulgar reference to death, and his grim embrace, was nothing compared with Jacques' tenacity just at this juncture. He held on with a stout heart. The horse, having more sense than his rider, as soon as he found his footing gone, swam for the shore, and came out with everything in good order, except Jacques, who found the panniers wrapped dangling about his neck, instead of being over the horses' back.

It took some moments to get matters righted before starting. Jacques enjoyed the interim in wringing out the tail of his threadbare coat. It was only with the practice of the utmost stoicism that I could refrain from laughter over this ludicrous scene.

The country beyond was overflown, and traveling, consequently, anything but safe or pleasant. The path, in leading back to the main route, ran through a low, wet, sedgy strip, for a distance of fully a mile. The mud in places was belly deep. My horses in several instances floundered, and could only be extricated by the rider dismounting. It was, therefore, with sensations of an exceedingly consolatory nature that I got back on the firm ground of the savannas. I had been obliged to help my own horse out of the mire on the way, so that I was now a fine sample of the fertile and adhesive mud of the Ozama.

At sunset I reached the Isabella, a tributary of the Ozama. The stream was exceedingly high. After leaving the high grounds, it was necessary to traverse a thick cane-break, knee deep with water, before coming to the borders of the main river.

Here I found a one-eyed ferryman, withered with years and of ebony blackness. The old fellow had just returned from the other side. His physical efforts were so great in this last voyage, that it required considerable coaxing and extra emolument, by way of encouragement, to bring matters to a satisfactory conclusion.

The river was bank full, and a hundred yards in width. It was by no means fordable. The negotiations between the ferryman and the diplomatic Jacques having favorably adjusted the points of difference, the horses were unpacked and unsaddled. The craft in which the crossing was to be effected, was a huge canoe, cut out of a log. In this, part of my traps were loaded. I took a seat in the bow, Jacques midships, and the ferryman, with his paddle, in the stern. The horses had to paddle their own canoe.

Everything being in readiness, the peon pushed the canoe from the shore, and drove the horses into the stream, while Jacques conducted them with a rope. Jacques' stupidity now very nearly was the means of a wreck on our voyage. Hardly had the canoe left the bank than the horse on the upper side drifted under the canoe. After giving the vagabond servant a whack over the head with my umbrella, as a gentle reminder of his fault in the impending disaster, I had him let go the one horse, and heading him up stream, soon got him extricated, and swimming back to the shore. The horse on the lower side was also turned back.

Having landed safely for a new start, I took charge of the horses myself. We once more pulled out into the stream. By a vigorous demonstration of my umbrella in the eyes of the horse on the upper side, I prevented a repetition of the occasion of the embarrassment in the first attempt. A small amount of yelling, also, to keep the animals at their work, soon found canoe, horses, and all landed on the opposite shore. The remainder of the baggage and packs, together with the peon and his horse, joined me without delay.

It was now growing dark with the accustomed rapidity of tropical latitudes. Hastily packing the animals, and having enlivened the ferryman with a few pieces of shining silver, I set out for the high-lands back from the river. At the suggestion of the peon, our gait was increased, in order to get out of the tangled brakes and dark, narrow gorges, or, I should say, deep furrows in the bluff side, before total darkness set in. The path through the brake was not more than six feet in width, and in some places, ascending the low hills bordering the rivers, it would have been impossible to ride two abreast, and yet this was within about ten miles of the capital.

It was with relief that I got out of the river bottom. The road now widened and ran beneath great vistas of overshadowing trees. *Maya* hedges and *palisars* were suggestive of cultivation.

Once more I had struck population. In the dim surrounding light I could observe that the attempts at agriculture were more elaborate than I had as yet seen.

I had determined to pass another night on the road, as I felt that it would be impossible to reach the capital before the closing of the gates. With this view, I despatched Jacques on his usual evening mission of diplomacy. After but a brief absence he returned with an explanation, that he had visited a house a short distance ahead, and that his reply from the only person there, a woman, was that her husband was not at home. What her husband had to do with a night's rest in his house was a puzzle. I made no further inquiries, but told the peon to hasten for San Carlos.

It was starlight, but not one of those bright ones produced by the twinkling eyes of night through our northern atmosphere. Still this was no obstruction to our progress, though I disliked extremely losing a sight of the country and habitations even on the remaining few miles of the road.

At about eight o'clock in the evening my sight was cheered by the lights of the suburban town of San Carlos, and in a few moments more we were within the limits of its habitations.

As I could now look down upon the lights of the capital, before settling for the night, I resolved to make an effort to enter. The Condé, one of the main gates, was at the foot of the hill. I set out on my experimental tour. Before reaching the bridge over the moat, a sentinel advanced and challenged. I halted and responded. Jacques, who was the prime minister of my establishment, advanced, and held a parley with the sentinel, who, in turn sent for the officer of the guard. With him I was enabled to make another advance as far as the very portals of the gate. With the officer here I held a parley myself, entertaining him with a synopsis of my journey and a few biographical points, backing up my statements with my passport. By way of a compromise, I suggested that he would send me and my attendants, under escort of a file of soldiers, to the Governor of the city.

The officer went off for an answer, probably, meanwhile sending off a courier to inform the Governor of what was going on, for it was fully fifteen minutes before he returned. Much to my satisfaction, the ponderous old-fashioned and clumsy gates ground their way about half open. My party filed in, and, taking the main street, headed for the hotel. After repeated challenges from the patrols, without serious delay, I dismounted in no ordinary frame of mental relief, in front of the Hotel du Commerce, in the capital of the republic. My advent was astounding to Mons. Auguste. He stood in the midst of the dining hall in mute astonishment. I soon aroused him from his reflections by turning the servants and animals over to him to be cared for.

My journey seemed, before the night was over, to be a subject of general comment throughout the city. Before I had time to remove my travel-stained apparel I had received several calls from acquaintances, civil and official. The President sent word that I was a true American; that my journey was a a remarkable one. but that Americans knew how to go ahead.

CHAPTER XXVI.

REFLECTIONS ON MY JOURNEY—A NOVEL METHOD OF GETTING RID OF MY SERVANT AND PEON—PLACES AND SUBJECTS OF INTEREST IN THE CAPITAL—THE CHURCH—THE CATHEDRAL—COLUMBUS' REMAINS.

A JOURNEY from Puerto Plata and Santiago de los Caballeros, to the Capital, is an experience which the traveler in San Domingo never repents having taken, as not worth the exposure, fatigues, and discomforts, necessary to its accomplishment. The trials of the journey are forgotten in the panoramic variety of landscape and points of interest and curiosity continually passing in view. Herds of fine horses and cattle, the wild hog bursting across the road-path into the thicket, the wild Guinea fowl timidly venturing from under cover in search of food, birds of every plumage at times, enliven the savannas or the forests. The *hattos* and small farms and villages, here and there, only at long intervals, bring up the scenes of desolation and bloodshed that have transformed a garden into a desert. Indeed everything is new, novel, and instructive.

The trip across the island, with all its natural attractions, and easily acquired, if need be, comforts, for travelers, is considered a great and dangerous undertaking. On this account, very few, whether people of the country or strangers, venture upon it, but prefer the tedious process of circumnavigating the island to the different ports, or to await the monthly American steamer, which now visits the island from New York, touching at the Capital, Samana bay, and Puerto Plata. As I was about starting from the north coast, I was gratuitously advised of the great and multifarious dangers of the journey, in addition to its discomforts. It was by some said to be a foolhardy attempt to penetrate alone into the interior. According to the accounts of these same authorities, everything was unsettled, revolutions were going on, the mountains were filled with refugees from justice, thieves, insurgents, and every other variety of hard cases, and the roads were beset with assassins and highway robbers; that my life or liberty would be uselessly jeopardized.

Such terrifying pictures were doubtless very serious subjects of contemplation to some, but my curiosity was all the more inflamed. I found a servant willing to accompany me; and a person, it is true, for almost the full value of the horses, willing to entrust three horses and a peon to me, for the journey. I carried my weapons in my valise, and set out entirely unarmed. For the benefit of these people, and for the world at large, in which the same opinions of diabolical scenes, hazards and cruelties, at every step, have become synonymous with San Domingo, I may say that I never experienced less sense of danger, received kinder treatment from the high, and greater respect from the low, than upon this very journey. Yet such are the erroneous impressions that have gone abroad with respect to the condition of San Domingo.

The day after my return to the capital I called upon the President, thanked him for the recognition that his own, and the letters of his ministers, had secured for me, and complimented him upon the order that prevailed in the interior. He very well replied: "We are very much misrepresented, and I am glad to find some one who has a practical knowledge of how false this all is. We have had our troubles, and there have been bloody times on the island.

But there is peace now, and, but for the conduct of a few ambitious leaders, our trouble would now be at an end."

My journey was not yet over. Having settled with the two worthies who had accompanied me, and having thrown in a few dollars to the peon, by way of *pour boire*, for himself, I found myself, suddenly, assumed of a responsibility which I had not anticipated. I had written several letters of thanks to my hospitable friends along my late line of travel, and was awaiting the arrival of Jacques and the peon, who were to depart the following noon. It was not until the second day that the individuals put in an appearance, and then in a state of such extreme intoxication that it was impossible to get anything intelligible out of either of them. Their return permits had already been arranged, which deprived them of that loophole of escape. The third day, still annoyed by their presence, as I felt them a responsibility as long as they were in the city, accepting a gentle suggestion, I informed both of the maudlin vagabonds, that if they were not off the same afternoon, I would have them put in the army. I have never met a Dominican, in the lower walks of life, who was in the army from choice. The effect of my verbal foray into their peace of mind had a magical and sobering effect. It was not over a hour after, that the two, for the fifth time, came to let me know they were off. As they departed, I repeated my terrifying resolution. They never more appeared.

I now felt free to devote the remainder of my time on the island, about eight days, to a more complete study of the points of interest at the capital city of the Republic, and also to make such investigations into the present condition of the island as would give a correct picture of its resources, government, trade, later history, and actual state of society. The most striking feature of the city of San Domingo is its numerous and extensive churches, and the ruins of the establishments formerly occupied by various religious orders. It seems, in the eye of a modern traveler, almost incredible, that in a city which, in its days of greatest prosperity, never numbered more than a population of twenty thousand souls, there should have been found the money and the labor to accomplish so much for the purposes of religion. It is certain that these vast outlays never came from the mother country, so that in this we have still another evidence of the enormous wealth and resources of the island.

The kingdom of religion here had its centre and

seat of power in the New World. In the year 1517, there was one bishopric at San Domingo, and one at La Vega. About 1527 these bishoprics were consolidated and made subject to the Archbishop of Seville. A few years later, the bishopric of San Domingo was raised to the dignity of an Archiepiscopal rank, having as suffragans, the Bishop of Cuba and Puerto Rico and the Abbot of Jamaica. The Archbishop was further dignified by the title, Primate of the Indies.

During the disturbances incident to the revolution the Church suffered materially. The people felt that the tyrannical interference and will of the Church in temporal affairs had been the cause of much of their sufferings, and had proved a bane upon the welfare of the city and the island. The churches were sacked and demolished, or were materially limited in their powers outside their proper sphere. It was not until 1813, after some years of neglect, that the Church again found a head in the person of Don Pedro Valera y Ximenes, who had been nominated by the regency of Spain, and was confirmed four years after.

In the days of religious splendor and potency, in addition to the strength of the Orders in the capital, there were Monastic institutions at Santiago, Azua, and San Juan. The monks were Dominicans, Franciscans, Mercenarians; the Nuns were Mercenarians, Capuchins, and of the orders of Regina Maria and Santa Clara. Upon the overthrow of Spanish supremacy, and the establishment of republican authority, by a decree of July 8, 1824, all the monasteries and nunneries were suppressed.

As an indication of the dignity and authority of the Church, the Archiepiscopal palace still stands, and at once strikes the visitor with surprise at the extent of its dimensions, and the lavish expenditure of time and means bestowed upon it. It is a stone building, square in plan, and constructed, after the Spanish style of architecture in use in its day. It has a court in the centre, from which a great stairway leads to the first floor. The building is extremely durable, and will yet last many years. From within its walls no longer go forth decrees of Rome to the faithful in all the Indies.

The most imposing religious structure of the city is the Cathedral, fronting on the southeast side of the Plaza. This massive pile of stone and mortar was founded in 1514, and finished in 1540. It is of Gothic design, architecturally, with towers and belfries. It is cruciform, nearly two hundred feet in length, and about ninety in width. The roof of the structure is remarkably durable, being constructed of brick laid in cement. It has resisted several earthquakes, and at the time of my visit, a bomb, thrown by an English ship during the bombardment of the city, was pointed out to me; it was but half buried in the hard roof. The bomb has been allowed to remain as a souvenir of those trying scenes.

Entering the immense structure by the main or west door, the lofty arches and pillars, and the elaborately carved altar, with its base of burnished silver, its candles, and gorgeous vases and flowers, the burning taper, and, indeed, all its trappings and ornaments, give an air of antiquity and solemnity, which inspires a sentimental reverence on the part of the stranger. The floors are of red brick, kept scrupulously clean. There are no seats in the cathedral, the worshipers being obliged to stand, or kneel, or sit on the floor.

From the body of the Cathedral lead off a number of side chapels, each devoted to a special saint, and having its appropriate forms of worship. In the first chapel, on the right hand side looking from the altar, I saw a massive sarcophagus in marble, with a life-size relief of its occupant, Bishop Elias, the founder of the Cathedral, in his full regalia, carved on the lid. In the second chapel, on the same side, is a painting, of great antiquity, of the Virgin. I here found an inscription, holding out the following inducement to Christian piety: "Most illustrious Señor Isidor Roongues, the metropolitan monarch of this metropolis, grants to all those that may pray before this image, for each paternoster, eight days of indulgence; other eight for every Ave Maria, and eight for each Gloria Patria Deo Gracia."

In one of the other side chapels I discovered, fastened against the wall, the cross Columbus planted upon the heights of Santo Cerro. The cross is about eight feet in height, and disguised by a modern innovation in the shape of a coat of green paint. The cross having been chipped by some unknown barbarians, it could be seen that the material, of which it is composed, is mahogany. Special services were dedicated to its honor.

There are six of these side chapels, extending on either side. At the west end of the cathedral is the shrine of San Michel, arrayed in armor. As the visitor stands on the right of the chancel, and gazes above a shrine to the Virgin, a small stone slab is visible high up in the main wall. Here, for over two centuries and a half, rested the remains of Christopher Columbus, the discoverer of the New World. Though his dust no longer rests there, the traveler feels an instinctive reverence for the sacred associations connected with the spot.

It may not be amiss, in this connection, to say a little about the remains of the discoverer of our hemisphere.

After a life, rendered immortal by the crowning achievement of all nautical skill and daring, his patron queen, the gentle Isabella, having died, the great services of Columbus were ignored. The cabals of intriguing men now met a ready ear at court. Upon the very island that he had contributed, the brightest jewel in the Spanish crown, he was seized and imprisoned in chains. Returning to Spain, to make his complaints, he was treated with indignity and rebuke. The ungrateful monarch paid no heed to his requests. Finding no sympathy, Columbus returned to Hispaniola. His restless and broken spirit here, amidst the scenes of his former grandeur and power, grieved the more. After a very brief sojourn (one month) on the island, with the Adelantado, his son, and servants, he once more embarked for Spain. The entire voyage was one of the most fearful he had ever experienced on the ocean, but an overruling Providence guarded him, and on November 7, 1504, he safely anchored in the harbor of San Lucar.

After lingering nearly two years, he died of neglect on May 20, 1506, at the advanced age of seventy years. As if, in his dying moments, feeling the ingratitude of man, his last words were a fitting tribute to his own nobility of soul: " Into thy hands, O Lord, I commend my spirit." The body was deposited in the convent of San Francisco, and the funeral obsequies were performed at Valladolid. In 1513, the remains were removed to the Carthusian monastery of Las Cuevas, of Seville. Here, also, were deposited the mortal remains of his son, Don Diego, on February 23, 1526. In 1536, the bodies of both Columbus and Don Diego were removed to Hispaniola. That of Columbus was placed in a small vault, built in the main wall, and on the right of the high altar. But the remains of the great discoverer were destined to be once more disturbed. The troubles of 1795, between France and Spain, resulted in the cession of the entire island of San Domingo to France. On the 11th of December, 1795, the commander of the Spanish squadron addressed a letter to Don Joaquin Garcia, Governor of San Domingo, respecting the remains of Columbus, lying in the great Cathedral. For reasons of national gratitude, for the good he had done to the State in his day, as well as for every other consideration that would naturally cluster about his memory, the Spanish commander requested to be permitted to remove the remains of Columbus and Don Diego to Cuba. The Archbishop of Cuba, to whose metropolis San Domingo belonged, had already given his consent. Accordingly on December 20, 1795, all the distinguished personages, civil and military, gathered in the great Cathedral to witness the disentombment of the remains, after they had lain in the vault for more than two hundred and fifty years. Upon opening the vault, within were found the pieces of a leaden coffin, a few bones, and the mould of a human body. These were collected and put in a gilded leaden case, about an half ell in length and breadth, and one-third in height, secured by an iron lock. The key, after the case was closed, was handed to the Archbishop. The case was placed in a coffin, covered with black velvet, and ornamented with lace, and fringe, and gold, and was put in a temporary mausoleum. A great gathering now took place, and a funeral sermon was preached in the Cathedral. With great ceremony the coffin was placed on the ship awaiting the precious dust. The key was handed by the Archbishop to the Commander of the Armada, to be given to the Governor of Havana. The ship sailed January 15, 1796.

The arrival of the dust was attended with appropriate forms, and with great pomp was conveyed to the Cathedral of Havana, and were deposited on the right side of the grand altar.

CHAPTER XXVII.

THE CONVENT OF SAN FRANCISCO—ALONZO DE OJEDA.

FROM the Cathedral I turned my steps towards the ruins of the Convent of San Francisco, in the northern part of the city. Next to the church of Santa Barbara, San Francisco occupied one of the chosen sites within the walls. It stood upon high ground, commanding a beautiful view. The walls of the convent and its tributary buildings, still afforded an idea of the enormous dimensions of the structure in the day in which it flourished. It occupied a large space of several acres, bounded on all sides by streets.

In approaching the ruins I came to an abrupt, though short, ascent, which conducted me, by a beaten path, to the main portal. The arched doorway and windows, as well as the wall, showed every sign of decay. As I entered the ruins I was set upon by a savage dog, in so unexpected a manner, that, at the first moment of the demonstration, I felt an inclination to retreat. A yell of disapprobation, and a postscript of irate Spanish, recalled the desperate canine, and at the same time had the good result of bringing me in intercourse with the old hag, who seemed to preside over the place. I was invited in, and having dropped an American half-dollar in her hand, she could not find sufficient ways in which to annoy me with attention, in addition to being of actual service in showing me about the ruin.

Within the court, as it appeared to have been originally, or, at all events, stepping within the main entrance, I found the enclosure bounded on all sides by high walls. A number of banana and cocoa-nut trees were growing there in a most thrifty condition. I also discovered a great number of rude bee-hives. The old woman seemed to consider that the bees were the most important features of the place, and set out in a lengthy discourse on bees and bee-raising, honey and bees-wax, until I was almost entirely diverted as regarded the historic structure which now surrounded me. However, I must admit one piece of useful intelligence gathered, and that was that Dominican bees have two seasons, instead of one, the swarming first, in May and June, and the second time in August.

From this enclosure I passed under the fragments of an arch, or dome, which towered high over head. This I was informed was the chapel. I was amazed at its dimensions, and the mechanical as well as architectural skill that must have been required to construct it. In looking towards the wall, in which the altar formerly stood, my reverence was considerably disturbed by the excessively comical air of a donkey, with his immense ears, standing in all the gravity of his species, in the small doorway near by. Here the feet of priests once passed, in solemn march to the altar. Here the reverential pageant and form of the Roman service was performed. Where the Host was once waved before the kneeling worshipers; where the incense was burned in recognition of the sanctity of the religion of Christ, is to-day a donkey-stall. Such is the incessant mutability, even in the outward circumstances of man's devotion to his God.

I spent some time in strolling among crumbled walls and broken pillars, overgrown with vine. I was more and more impressed with the size of the establishment, and the vast outlays, from some source, it must have required to keep it up.

Returning to the main doorway, I was pointed out the grave of the heroic Alonzo de Ojeda. I halted under the crumbling portal in which he was buried, and stood upon the now traceless tenement of this chivalric man.

Of all the adventurous spirits, who figured in the eventful period of maritime history, immediately succeeding the greatest enterprise of Columbus, none were more earnest, none more brave, none more gallant, than this same Alonzo de Ojeda. In San Domingo, his name is the household word for human daring, human suffering, human endurance, and human misfortune. One of the most enthusiastic and resolute followers of the great Admiral, in his earliest voyages, the name of Alonzo de Ojeda beams upon the opening pages of the thrilling records of discovery and exploration, on the island of Hispaniola itself, as well as of the unknown seas, and shores of countries peopled with a fierce and savage race. It is because his life is a part of the dawning history of San Domingo; because, from constant disasters, he returned there to start afresh with unabated zeal; because his eventful career ended there, and his body is buried there, under circumstances and amid surroundings of such striking interest, that the story of his career, so full of the thrill of romance, and typical of that class of actors on the world's drama, is worthy of a place here.

A native of Cuença, New Castile, and of reputable parentage, as page in the service of Don Luis de Cerda, Duke of Medina Celi, one of the most powerful nobles of Spain, Alonzo gathered his first lessons to fit him for the sphere in history which he afterwards so completely filled. In the wars against the Moors, in Granada, so perfect a school in training up the leaders in the events of the New World, Alonzo followed his master, and frequently elevated himself above his companions by the glory and daring of his deeds. It is recorded of him, as among his early acts of coolness and courage, that the Queen, with her royal suite, being in the tower of the great cathedral of Seville, known as Giralda, Ojeda, for their amusement, mounted a beam reaching out a distance of twenty feet, like an arm, and, walking to the end, poised himself on one leg.

In physique, Ojeda was small, but possessed extraordinary strength, and a constitution capable of surmounting the severe tests to which it was exposed. In the use of the weapons of the day, he had no superior. Thus qualified, the deeds that he accomplished were worthy of his manly spirit.

It is told of him, that in all his expeditions, whether by sea or land, he carried with him a Flemish painting of the Holy Virgin. This was one of the pious contributions of a priestly relative, Don Juan Rodriguez Fonseca. Ojeda, in common with all his fellow-adventurers, possessed a certain kind of religious fervor, which buoyed him up under many trying circumstances. Whether in the deep and dark forests of the Cibao, or whether in the distant thickets of Carthagena, night and morning, before his treasured painting, suspended against a tree, he bent the knee in making his solemn orisons. Preceding every dangerous undertaking, the smiles of the Holy Virgin were invoked, and, in times of excessive trial, he applied to it the pious antidote of repeated vows, in hopes of outliving his troubles in order to perform them.

It was Ojeda who first visited the mountain dominions of the Cacique Caonabo, and enjoyed, before all his companions, the delightful vision of the interior. His glowing accounts of the beautiful country, and rivers abounding in gold, excited the curiosity and cupidity of Columbus. The Admiral and four hundred men, in battle armor, with lance and arquebuse, and banners streaming, led by Ojeda, visited the country which the bold explorer had already viewed, and from the heights of Santo Cerro drank in the inspiration of the gorgeous prospect of the Vega.

It would be impossible here more than merely to allude to the chain of startling experiences that formed the life of the gallant Alonzo de Ojeda. He had already characterized his courage, at arms, and skill in battle, by his stubborn conflicts with the overwhelming legions of Caonabo. His civil administration of the affairs of the interior of the island, against the intrigues of envious rivals, was as decisive as the charges of his invincible and dashing cavaliers upon the valor of native warriors. Nor did his spirit of adventure prompt him alone to engage in well-supported contests. We have already learned of his unheard-of daring in visiting the terrible Mountain King, and reciprocating his hospitality and confidence by carrying him captive to the rejoiced community at Isabella. But the restless spirit that burned within the panting breast of Ojeda could no longer brook the narrow limits of a single island. He longed to be upon the broad ocean, to seek new latitudes, to turn over the still uncut leaves of geographical knowledge, to spread the arms of his country, to advance the cause of religion, to conquer new people, and to colonize strange lands. With these great thoughts and ambitions evolving in his his mind, he returned to his native Spain and presented himself, the supplicant of new hardships and fresh dangers.

The fame of Ojeda, in the New World, had gone before him; the little examples of his youth were refreshed by the achievements of his maturer years; these, combined with the assistance of influential friends, and the willing ear of his Sovereign, Ojeda had little difficulty in securing the goal for which he sought.

Columbus, having discovered the coast of Paria, Ojeda was commissioned to explore it. His proud spirit did not wish to follow in the footsteps of a predecessor, but curbing, for an instant, his feeling, he saw here the opening to that greater field which his imagination had spread out before him.

In May, 1499, Ojeda sailed for Port St. Mary. As if caring little, after he had cut loose from the orders of his superiors, he struck the New World, two hundred leagues further south than his master, Columbus, and thus began his own eventful career as a discoverer.

Ojeda now sailed along the coast, and discovered the rivers Esquivo and Oronoko, he touched at Trinidad and the Gulf of Paria, and, passing through the

Straits of the Boca del Drago, or Dragon's Mouth, steered along the *terra firma*, until he arrived at Curiana, or the Gulf of Pearls. At Maracapano he built a brigantine. We also find him here, at the request of the natives, embarking in a crusade against their cannibal neighbors. For this purpose, he took seven of the people of the country, and after a seven days' voyage, through a chain of islands, supposed to be the Carribee, arrived in the hostile country. The fierce warriors, painted, and armed, and undismayed, came down to the shore to meet him. Ojeda, anchoring his ships, lowered several boats; in one placing a cannon, and in each a number of soldiers, secreted in the bottom, he pulled for the shore. The enraged savages, assailing with their rude instruments of opposition, threw themselves into the sea to prevent his landing. Suddenly the Spaniards rose up in their boats. Terrified at the discharge of the cannon and arquebuses, the warriors fled back on the land. Ojeda, landing his men, pursued the fugitives on the land.

The next day Ojeda landed with a stronger force and destroyed their houses, after which he re-embarked and sailed back to the mainland with his booty and captives. He continued his adventurous voyage along the coast, reaching Curacoa, according to the early explorers, inhabited by a race of giants. Continuing on his course, he reached a great bay. He saw a number of bell-shaped houses, built on piles. Each house was provided with a draw-bridge and canoes, This was literally a city of the sea, and owing to this fact, Ojeda named it the Gulf of Venice, and the town Venezuela, or, Little Venice. The population abandoned their homes upon the approach of Ojeda, and took refuge on shore. Soon after sixteen young girls were brought down to propitiate the strangers. They were distributed among the ships. The natives now came off, and the greatest harmony prevailed. Suddenly a signal was given. The girls jumped into the sea, and the Indians in the canoes, and in the water, produced their warlike weapons and began an attack. Their futile efforts, however, were soon overcome, and the fierce Coquibacoans were now seeking protection in the forests on the land.

We next find our hero visiting San Domingo, but being refused a landing on the island, returned to Spain.

CHAPTER XXVIII.

THE STORY OF ALONZO DE OJEDA—CONTINUED.

IN 1502, we find Ojeda again in Venezuela, raising the arms of Spain in token of possession. Not satisfied with the country, which had the appearance of sterility, he pursued the coast to Bahai Honda. Here he was amazed to find a white man, but upon inquiry it turned out to be a Spaniard, left there thirteen months before, by Bastides, and who had, in these moments of isolation among savages, and in a savage land, acquired the language.

Factions now broke out among the explorers. Ojeda was put in irons and carried to Hispaniola. While sailing along close to the shore, he let himself over the ship's side to swim ashore, but his feet being shackled, he was compelled to cry for help, and was again taken on board.

Reaching San Domingo, his rivals accused him of every crime, and being brought to a trial, he was deprived of all his property, and also found himself deeply in debt. Although, in the following year, his appeals to his sovereign were answered by an order for a restitution of his property, the litigation in which his affairs had been involved had consumed it all.

We hear nothing more of Ojeda for several years, but his restless spirit was not idle. His mind was constantly filled with new schemes of adventure. A new expedition, under Ojeda and Nicuesa, was arranged. Although penniless, through the assistance of a friend, he was enabled to contribute his share in the expenses. This friend was Martin Fernandez de Encisco, a bachelor, who put all his money in the enterprise, with the understanding that he was to be Alcalde and Chief Judge for the Government. Ojeda was to go on the expedition, and the bachelor was to remain, for the present, to look after its interests in Hispaniola.

Two such spirits as Ojeda and Nicuesa could not long thrive together. Jamaica had been assigned to them in common. Nicuesa was disposed to settle the difficulties in an amicable way, but Ojeda, more hot-headed, swore that he would bring terms with the sword, and offered, in addition, to stake five thousand castillanos, on the result, in his favor. Through the interposition of Juan de la Cosa, a brave man and a friend of Ojeda, a conflict was avoided.

Don Diego Columbus was next appealed to, and took the matter in his own hands. He ordered Juan de Esquibel to take possession of Jamaica. This order so infuriated Ojeda, that he drew his sword, and, waving it in the face of Don Diego, threatened that he would strike off the head of Esquibel if he should ever meet him on the island.

In November, 1509, Ojeda sailed from San Domingo with two ships, two brigantines, and three hundred men. With him was the daring Francisco Pizarro, later the Conqueror of Peru. After a favorable voyage, the ships landed in the harbor of Carthagena. They were at once met by the hostile demonstrations of the natives, who came out, the men brandishing their palm-wood swords, and the women flourishing their lances.

With his customary impetuosity, Ojeda landed with a few men. As if to observe a show of formality, the friar read a proclamation. In response, the natives set up a dismal sound of conches. This performance was just of a character to spur on the reckless ire of Ojeda. He assailed the savages, and followed them to their strongholds in the forest, to the cry of St. Jago.

Having destroyed their town, and supposing the natives defeated, the Spaniards separated in search of booty. The undismayed warriors soon rallied, and, assailing the Spaniards at this disadvantage, got the better of them. Ojeda took refuge within a native enclosure. The savages here pursued him. La Cosa, a brave and determined companion, came to his succour. The fierce warriors were kept at bay. Ojeda, seeing the desperation of the occasion, sprang upon the assailants with the strength of an infuriated lion. With his sword he cut right and left, dealing death in all directions. Of his companions in the enclosure, only one out of seventy escaped.

Ojeda failed to reach the ship. His companions, unable to discover him among the corpses of his followers, in the severe contest on shore, did everything, in the way of search and signaling, in order to obtain some tidings of their lost leader. As they were about to abandon the search, a party discovered a human body lying in a mangrove thicket near the beach. It was Ojeda. He had taken refuge there, and, unable to get away, was nearly famished. When found, he was lying upon the ground, and, though nearly dead, held his sword in his hand as if waiting for some new encounter.

While these unfortunate events were transpiring, Nicuesa, the rival of Ojeda, arrived in the bay. Ojeda, rescued from his desperate situation, had no thoughts of encountering Nicueso. But that brave adventurer was not of a revengeful spirit. He received Ojeda in open arms, and the two, uniting their forces, again attacked the savages on shore. They surrounded their chief stronghold, and destroyed it, with all its occupants.

The next we hear of Ojeda, is in founding the colony of San Sebastian, on the Gulf of Uraba. In one of his conflicts with the natives of this wild region, Ojeda was wounded with a poisoned arrow. A story is told of him on this occasion, which shows the character of the man. He had seen his companions fall beneath the subtle influences of poison inflicted by the weapons of the natives. Knowing what his own fate would be, if not attended to, Ojeda had two suitable pieces of iron heated red-hot. One of these, he ordered his surgeon to apply to each opening of the wound. The surgeon, fearing to use the desperate remedy, declined to obey, saying that he would not be the murderer of his commander. Ojeda, enraged at the opposition, threatened that he should be hanged if he did not do as he was bid. The remedy was applied, and, after days of intense suffering, Ojeda was again able to lead his men.

. The condition of the colony soon gave rise to disorders. Starvation stared the adventurers in the face. Leaving Francisco Pizarro in command, with liberty to abandon the place if no tidings reached him in fifty days, Ojeda set out for San Domingo for fresh supplies. On the way the men on board the ship broke out in open mutiny. Ojeda was seized and put in irons. This insult enraged his fierce spirit beyond measure. Shaking his chains at his persecutors, he offered to fight each one successively if they would only give him a clear deck. There were none on board who were willing to try the experiment. A fearful storm broke upon the ocean. The mutineers were now glad enough to unchain Ojeda if he would navigate the vessel. But the storm remained unabated, and in their hopeless situation they were compelled to run the vessel in, and land on the coast of Cuba.

From here the party set out in hopes of reaching Hispaniola. On the way, meeting with great opposition from fugitives from Hayti, they abandoned the high country and pursued their journey through interminable marshes. Sometimes they traveled waist deep in water, and at night were compelled to climb trees for a dry place to sleep. Their situation now grew worse than ever. Some of the party fell by the way, utterly exhausted, and were left to die. Ojeda, as a last and crowning act of pious supplication and sacrifice, produced his Flemish picture of the Virgin, and offered that great treasure as a propitiatory inducement, declaring that he would build a chapel at the first village, and leave the picture in it, if he should be spared.

The resolution about the picture had the desired effect, at least, probably, so thought the now less enthusiastic Ojeda. The party reached an Indian village. They were kindly received, and the Cacique sent out and brought in the rest of the party, stragling in exhaustion, or dying along the road. Ojeda and his companions unexpectedly found themselves transmuted, in the minds of the natives, into a band of angels, and were, in consequence, accorded due honors and appropriate acts of reverence and devotion.

Ojeda kept his promise. He built the chapel, and with a final pang of repentance for his rashness, left the companion and consolation of his trials, the Flemish picture. The chapel was long after the resort of the people for the performance of the offices of the religion of Ojeda. A few natives, in the boats of the country, were sent to Jamaica to ask succor. Here was Juan de Esquibel in command, the very one whose head Ojeda threatened to strike off. This piece of thoughtless temper seems to have been entirely forgotten, or at least suppressed, for we hear that not only did Esquibel send over one of his own caravals to bring away the unfortunate party, but Ojeda, upon landing, was received in the most friendly manner.

By the first craft Ojeda set out for San Domingo. Arriving at the city he found his patron, the bachelor, had sailed with supplies for the colony of San Sebastian. His friend away, and himself once more a victim of misfortune, the treatment which Ojeda now received was cold and distant. One night, he was fiercely assailed by the friends of Talavera, a pirate, who had been taken and hanged, and against whom Ojeda had appeared as a witness. His assailants being too strong in numbers, Ojeda placed his back against a wall, and, with his quick and powerful sword, he warded off the desperate demonstrations directed against him, and wound up by putting the whole party to flight, and pursuing them through the streets of the city.

This was the last act preceding the giving way of the proud and manly Alonzo de Ojeda. His life of hardships and disappointments had told severely upon him. He was broken in spirit and empty in purse. The discoverer of empires, the "servant of the high and mighty Kings of Castile and Leon, civilizer of barbarous nations, their messenger and captain," was now a vagrant in the streets of San Domingo, shunned by the rich, and scorned by the poor. With no heart to rise out of his humiliation, and with no prospects to enter some mission of inevitable death, it is said he turned monk, and entered the Convent of San Francisco. This is not authenticated by history. But it is true, that Alonzo de Ojeda died so poor and friendless, that he had not enough to pay for his burial. At a lucid interval in the delirium, preceding mortal dissolution, with gasping breath, he beseeched that his body might be buried in the main portal of the Convent of San Francisco, "that every one who entered there might tread upon his grave, and be reminded of the instability of human fortune."

CHAPTER XXIX.

THE CHURCHES OF SAN DOMINGO—RUINS—REMAINS OF THE PALACE OF DON DIEGO COLUMBUS—THE PUBLIC BUILDINGS—A MARKET SCENE—COLUMBUS' WELL—THE LEGEND OF THE GOLDEN COMB.

AFTER visiting the Cathedral and the Convent of San Francisco I took the remaining places, now, or formerly, devoted to religious purposes, as was most convenient. The Church of San Domingo, situated near the sea-front of the city, I found in a good state of preservation, and still devoted to the observances of religion. The structure was large, and when the authority, spiritual and temporal, was in the full blaze of glory on the island, the Church of San Domingo evidently absorbed a large share of the substantial piety of the people. Its gray walls and time-worn cornices and towers, the antique bells in the belfry, all pointed out the Church of San Domingo as one of the very earliest religious establishments. The Convent of San Domingo, formerly connected with the church, has been abandoned.

I will merely give the names of the other places for religious purposes, and now in use: the Church of Santa Barbara, near the bastion of Santa Barbara, at one of the extreme northern angles of the city walls; the Chapel of Las Remedios, near the President's Palace; Chapel of San Lazro, and hospital for lepers, immediately inside the northwestern wall; Chapel of Carmen, in the southwestern part of the city, and Chapel of San Andros, adjoining; Chapel Regina Angelorum, near the sea-wall, and the American chapel, facing the sea, at the bastion of San Fernando.

The religious establishments now closed, or in ruins, are the chapel of San Antonio, inside the northwest wall, near the bastion of San Antonio; the chapel of San Nicholas, about the heart of the city; La Merced convent, on the main street of the city, about midway between the two gates; the convent of Santa Clara, in the southeastern corner of the city, near the citadel; the old Archiepiscopal Palace near the church of San Domingo. Across the river, on the site of the first town, stands the chapel of Columbus. It is very small, and was the first built after it was determined to erect a city at the mouth of the Ozama. In the modern city is also a chapel, built by Columbus, in a remarkably fine state of preservation. Near by is the sun-dial of Columbus, consisting of a column of brick, twelve feet in height, with the dials so adjusted as to be seen from the pedestal. The dial is still used.

The college of Jesuits is also a fine building, notwithstanding the dilapidation into which it has fallen. It is now used as a theatre. The edifice is massive in its proportions, and in the manner in which it is constructed. It stands across the street from a building formerly used as the President's Palace.

Judging from the extent and numbers of the buildings set apart for the exercise of the various functions of Government, it appears that in early days, next to religion, this branch of power engaged the attention of the larger share of the better class, and absorbed immensely the substance of the people. In this we find another cause of the abject poverty and oppression which constantly prevailed, and, together with other circumstances, is and will be, until a change be made, an entail upon the population. When religion and government go united, with greedy hands, to rob the people, it is not surprising that the whole structure falls. It is no wonder that the people, unwilling to endure a lot subservient to the extravagance and luxury of a class, rose in rebellion. It is equally no cause of surprise that those who suffered by the fall, practised such unheard of excesses and barbarities, before yielding into the hands of the governed.

Near the bastion of Don Diego stands an edifice, conspicuously exposed to view from the Ozama. It is known as the ruins of the Palace of Don Diego Columbus. Unlike his father, Don Diego was prone to imitate the extravagant example set by Castilian notions. After considerable delay and litigation, the father being dead, the son succeeded in having Ovando, the Governor of San Domingo, recalled, and was himself sent out to rule the colony. In June, 1509, Don Diego sailed for Hispaniola, taking with him his new wife, Dona Maria de Teledo, daughter of the Grand Commander of Leon, his brother, Don Fernando, his two uncles, Don Bartholomew and Don Diego, a retinue of cavaliers, and a number of young ladies of rank. His powers were not fully that of Viceroy, but his wife was always recognized as the Vice Queen.

Upon his arrival at the capital, Don Diego, with

the assistance of the great and noble men and women, he had brought with him, established a miniature court. The Government of Hispaniola now reveled in the luxury of the trappings and reality of regal sway on a small scale. Great ceremonies, and occasions of formal display, were the order of thë day. Diego, surrounded by these fascinations, almost forgot the responsibilities of his position. Not satisfied with the buildings occupied by the former Governors, Don Diego began a new and more commodious one, which, had it been completed, would have ranked in dimensions with any of the other large buildings of the city. To-day the walls of the palace are entire; but all the wood-work has gone to decay, and it is also roofless. The interior is overgrown with wild vine and weeds.

The erection of this building gave considerable trouble, and in connection with other points of controversy disturbed the administration of Don Diego. Factions sprung up, and he was continually harrassed. He visited Spain in 1515, and returned in 1520, only to find the island even in greater confusion. In 1523 he was rebuked by the Council of the Indies, and returned to Spain. He never went back to the island.

The public buildings, formerly occupied by the

government, present the best exhibition of the extravagant notions of the people of the island several centuries ago, and even down to the last tread of Spanish dominion.

The citadel and barrack, signal tower, and arsenal, cover a large space in the southeastern part of the town, on the point overlooking the mouth of the river. All these buildings, with slight repairs, would be fit for use. The barracks are capable of quartering from fifteen to twenty thousand troops. The tower, at the extreme point of land, is connected with the time of Columbus' humiliation. It was here that he was in chains before being sent to Spain. The same structure is now used as a signal tower, for approaching vessels, and a prison for political offenders. The tower shows no signs of decay.

Among the buildings belonging to the government, for civil purposes, are the National Palace, the President's Palace, but not now occupied by Baez, the Palace of the Congress, and the Municipal Buildings. All these structures are commodious, and were used for governmental purposes by the Spaniards. The city of San Domingo is the military as well as the civil centre of the Republic.

Near the National Palace, and but a few minutes

walk from the Bastion Don Diego, is the marketplace, a large open square, containing a number of low sheds, and surrounded by shops. Frequently, during my presence in the city, early in the morning, I visited this scene of bustle and activity. The space was crowded with people of all ages, sexes, and conditions. The purchasers were generally men, while the sellers were mostly women. The latter sat upon stools, and had their articles for sale displayed upon mats spread upon the ground. The market sheds were used by large dealers, and particularly by butchers.

The confusion of sounds, and the different degrees of temper exhibited on these occasions, were almost distracting. A few pennies worth of ginger-root, for instance, would elicit the most earnest appeals from the seller, which were invariably met by the most emphatic denunciations of extortion by the purchaser. Take several hundred of such dialogues and some idea may be formed of the harmony of sounds produced, on a market morning, in San Domingo.

The abundance and variety of the productions brought in was large. With the indigenous fruits of the country, were the vegetables of our own latitude, in their season.

The Well of Columbus, situated about a quarter of a mile above the city, on the banks of the Ozama, is also a place of considerable curiosity to strangers visiting San Domingo city. Originally, the Well was dug for the use of vessels taking in water for a sea-voyage, and it is frequently used for the same purpose at the present day. It is covered with a substantial, arched building of brick, about twelve feet in length and six in width, and stuccoed. It is built well back in the hill-side. The Well is about three feet deep, with a stone bed. The arch-covering over head is about twelve feet high. In front of the building, is a large stone basin, with conduits from within for the water to pass out from the Well. The basin is also surrounded by a low wall, which forms a sort of court. Judging from these arrangements, the Well, at one time, must have yielded a higher level of water, as the basin, when I saw it, was entirely dry, and appeared as if it had not been used for years. The water in the Well was cool and sweet, indeed particularly refreshing, after a tramp through the smothering foliage along the river bank.

While seated beneath the grateful shade of a beautiful mango, my companion repeated a brief story, much in vogue amongst the people, in connection with the Well. He called his story THE LEGEND OF THE GOLDEN COMB:

Upon the return of the son of Miguel Diaz and Zameaca, the Queen of the Ozamas, from Spain, about 1520, the young man found that his mother had disappeared. The Indian natives looked upon him as a prince, and, almost immediately, planned a conspiracy to place him at their head as ruler. The conspiracy was discovered, and quelled with great severity. The leaders sought refuge from the blood-thirsty vengeance of the Spaniards. Near the city was a famous retreat, known as the Water Cave, because it was necessary to dive into a lake in order to get into it. To this place a number of chiefs fled, and eluded discovery. In the service of the Governor's wife was a beautiful slave girl. Her mistress, to secure her veil, wore a very valuable golden comb. The slave girl had long felt a desire to possess the comb. One day she told her mistress how happy she would be, if she would give her the comb. Her mistress, discovering this weakness, at once replied that she would give it to her if she would show the Governor of the island where the Indian chiefs were secreted. The slave girl had a lover who was one of the conspirators. She said, if he would be released, she would then tell the secret. Her mistress assured her that her lover should be pardoned, and that the golden comb would be laid on the altar, and she should take it as soon as the retreat of the chiefs was discovered.

A trusty attendant of the Governor was selected to go with the slave girl. She led him through a hidden path, which could only be discovered by one familiar with its course. At last they came to the banks of the lake, in front of the cave. Having secreted her companion, the slave girl seated herself on the margin of the lake, and began to sing a sort of chant, known as the signal to the occupants of the cave. While the plaintive strains were still stealing through the quiet air, the form of an aged man appeared out of the bosom of the placid lake.

Daily the native women came with food, and in the same way signalled to those within the cave, when a few came out and secured the food, and passed it to their companions. The slave girl conversed with the old man, and they separated.

The Governor's spy was satisfied. The two returned to the city, and communicated what had transpired. A number of soldiers were now sent, and, ready to pounce upon the betrayed chiefs, were posted in secret places. The slave girl sang the fatal chant, several chiefs came out, and were seized.

One of the chiefs, before he was executed, spied the slave girl who had betrayed him. He said, pointing to her, "I now go to a land of peace; you will never find the way there." The next of the chiefs were either taken and executed, or starved to death in the cave, rather than come out and meet the cruel fate which awaited them at the hands of their oppressors.

The lover of the slave was among the number taken. When he found how the betrayal was accomplished, he cursed the once-object of his affection. The girl, realizing the fearful calamity she had brought upon her people, died of grief.

Tradition says, that after the destruction of the fugitives, at a certain time every year, during the evening, the figure of a woman, with a golden comb, can be seen weeping on the margin of the lake, at the mouth of the cave.

CHAPTER XXX.

THE FATE OF ANACAONA, QUEEN OF XARAGUA.

NEAR the northeastern angle of the city walls stands an immense tree, called *Saiba* by the people. The trunk measured, at least, eight feet in diameter, while the branches reached out to an enormous distance. The tree, according to the accounts given of it, was connected with at least two events in the history of the island. I was informed that it marks the spot where the first slaves brought to San Domingo were landed. As this occurred in 1512, at the time of my visit the tree had been standing at least three hundred and fifty years.

I was also told that, under this tree, Anacaona, the beautiful Queen of Cibao, met her melancholy end. The story was told me by a lady now residing in

San Domingo city. I will give the facts, as nearly as possible, as they came from her lips.

Anacaona was famed among natives, as well as Spaniards, as a woman of remarkable beauty, and surpassing dignity and grace of manner. She was far above the mass of her sex, and, with her husband, the ill-fated Caonabo, shared the responsibilities and honors of regal sway. When the mighty chieftain was deserted by his warriors, and a captive in the hands of the white fiends, Anacaona assumed command of the shattered army, and rallying her subjects took a stand for a desperate, and as it proved, a fruitless defence. Several caciques had combined in this patriotic war. Manicaotex, brother of Caonabo, Guarionex, Cacique of the Royal Vega, and Behechio, the brother-in-law to Caonabo, had their warriors marshaled on plain and in forest, in a vain effort to stem the tide of invasion, tyranny, servitude, and extermination.

The day was fatal to the allied armies. At a timely moment, in the crisis of the strife, Alonzo de Ojeda, with his invincible steel-clad and bristling cavalry, like messengers of death and destruction, fell upon the naked cohorts of the enemy. The contest was decided in one fell swoop. The armies broke and fled to the fastnesses of the mountains.

The caciques readily yielded submission, except Behechio, who, with his sister, the beautiful wife of Caonabo, retired to his own dominions, in the extreme southwestern parts of the island.

Xaragua, for such was the native name of the dominions of Behechio, was unexcelled by any part of the beautiful land of Hayti. The climate possessed unequalled salubrity, the vegetation exhibited all the varied forms and colors incident to the most attractive and endless productions of tropical latitudes, the people were a finer type than were found in other parts of the island, and were graced with manners both gentle and kind.

By the remoteness of their abodes the people had not suffered from the vile contamination which attended the presence of the licentious throng of adventurers, who had gathered from Spain. These happy people sang their areyots, or legendary ballads, they joined in their national games and dances in the palm groves, and, influenced by the mild and maternal spirit of Anacaona, were in every respect the most fortunate and happy of people.

But this state of national felicity was not destined to continue long. The downfall of the avenging caciques of the Cibao, and the Royal Vega, opened the way and invited the further aggression of the

Spaniards. No sooner had the Adelantado established himself at the then new city of San Domingo than, leaving twenty men to guard the city, he sallied forth on a visit to the distant abode of the people of Behechio.

Notwithstanding the deep sorrow Anacaona had experienced in the sufferings of the subjects of her consort, and the more poignant grief sustained in the uncertain fate that had attended her heroic husband, after his captivity, this remarkable woman displayed that magnanimity of soul that sacrificed the bitter impulse of revenge to the interests of the weak.

In addition to her physical beauty, Anacaona was gifted with a sweetness of disposition, which enabled her to exercise great influence, both over her brother and his subjects. She had also rendered her name a cherished thing all over the island, by the composition of ballads, which, in their hours of peaceful recreation, the natives sang.

Her name Anacaona, " the golden flower," signified her angelic purity of person and heart. Anacaona knew the power of the Spaniards. She therefore, when she heard of the approach of the Adelantado, pressed her brother to abandon his vindictive spirit, and to strive to conciliate the strangers.

The Adelantado, in all the "pomp and circumstance" of military array, moved through the country. About thirty leagues on the way, he reached the banks of the Neyva. Here, Behechio, against the wishes of his sister, had formed in hostile force. The Adelantado was, however, too well supported. Glistening helmets and cuirasses, contrasting with the naked bodies of his troops, led Behechio to a different decision. He now laid aside his weapons, and disbanding his army, went forward to meet the Adelantado. Everything was in hurry and confusion. Messengers were sent to the capital to make preparations for the reception of the guest. Where but a few hours before all was painful anxiety and distracting despair, there now reigned mirth and willing preparation. Anacaona, relieved of her dismal forebodings, with womanly ingenuity, joined in, to touch the tender chords of the hearts of the strangers.

The rest of the journey was an ovation. Along the way the tributary Caciques furnished great loaves of cassava, and fruits in profusion and endless variety.

The capital of Behechio was situated on a high swell of ground overlooking the placid waters of a beautiful bay.

As the distinguished guest approached, Anacaona, attended by thirty females of her brother's household, met the regal party. Their mild voices sang areyots, framed from the genius of their queenly leader; they danced and waved immense palm leaves. The married women wore richly embroidered aprons, extending almost to the knees. The maidens were entirely naked. Their raven locks fell in graceful tresses upon their shoulders. Upon their heads they wore fillets of gold. Their beautifully moulded forms, their delicate skin, of a pale brown, struck the strangers with astonishment. The scene was calculated to soothe for the moment the hellish passions of the throng of adventurers. What a contrast! What a picture of the wide extremes of human nature! Anacaona, surrounded by all that was divine in form and purpose!—the proud Adelantado and his highly caparisoned followers, with hearts and hands died in atrocities, that had caused rivers of blood to spring from a people striving against diabolical tyranny and fiendish injustice!

As Don Bartholomew drew near, the female attendants fell upon their knees, and having performed obeisance, handed him flowers, brought for the occasion. When this ceremony was concluded, Anacaona, reclining upon a rustic litter, borne by six natives, was brought into the presence of the Adelantado. She wore but a simple apron. Upon her angelic brow rested garlands of tropical flowers, only dimmed by the radiance of her own beauty. Upon her neck and arms were other floral tributes.

Thus Anacaona, "The Golden Flower," received the Adelantado, Don Bartholomew Columbus, and his followers into the province of Xaragua.

For two days mirth reigned—an elysium of repose from the hardships of warlike toil. The Adelantado occupied the great house of the Cacique. An immense banquet was given. Utias, fish, roots and fruits, were provided in abundance. The Adelantado, from the hands of the charming Anacaona, overcame his repugnance for the serpent-like guana. All followed the Adelantado's example, and the guana henceforth became the coveted dainty of the Spanish epicure. National games and dancing followed. The festivities terminated in a sham battle, in which four natives were slain and many wounded. The stubborn and serious contest was only suspended at the urgent request of the Adelantado.

The object of the visit was now made known to Behechio and Anacaona. Behechio, anticipating this, promptly responded that he knew it was gold that they wanted, but that that was not found in his territory. The Adelantado replied, that he could not expect what was not to be found, but the Cacique might pay his tribute in cassava bread, hemp, and cotton. To this Behechio agreed, and at once ordered all his tributary chieftains to furnish, at the proper times, the necessary supplies.

Thus, peaceably, the Adelantado found himself in authority over one of the most charming and productive territories on the island. Bidding farewell to his royal host, he now returned to the seat of his own official power.

Such was the opening of a period of blasted hopes, of dire sufferings. As the flames of oppression lashed stronger and more fierce, we find, in its most atrocious form, the molten wrath of human depravity emptied upon a defenceless and confiding people, to devour them.

Not long after the first visit of the Adelantado, Roldan, an aspiring and reckless Spaniard, hoisted the standard of rebellion. Taking advantage of the instinctive hostility of the natives, he made propositions to them, espousing their cause against the tyrannical sway, as it was exercised by the then authorities.

As the result of listening to his words, the natives soon found themselves, more than ever, ruined. At last, this unscrupulous adventurer withdrew to Xaragua, where he domiciled himself, in opposition to the authority of the island.

After a sad chapter of disaster and rapid decline, we find Behechio dead, and the beautiful Anacaona his successor, as Queen, invested with all his regal powers, his estate, and, sadder than all, the incumbent cares and racking anxieties of those unhappy days. The Queen had been the friend of the strangers. The unfortunate passion of Fernando de Guevara for her daughter, Higuenamota, combined with the inexorable rapacity of the Spaniards, wrought a great change in the feelings of Anacaona. She no longer exercised that kind hospitality. Yet she fully realized her inability to do more than, by peaceable instruments, to attempt to stay the daily increasing oppression and licentiousness practised by the strangers. The crimes of the miserable fugitives who resorted to her dominions, were charged against the Queen. Thus harrassed on all sides, the melancholy fate of herself and her people seemed to be hastening on with relentless and irresistible march.

The reckless outrages of the arrogant and grasping Bobadilla, were only exceeded by the perverse Nicholas de Ovando, his successor in the rule of Hispaniola. This heartless worthy had scarcely seated himself in the chair of authority, than he turned his malicious eye upon the beautiful regions of Xaragua. Already, extreme unhappiness reigned there, but it was the lot of this man to crown the structure.

In 1503, at the head of three hundred foot and seventy horse, Ovando set out for the dominions of the Queen. This treacherous dignitary pretended that it was a visit of friendship. The Queen, notwithstanding her bitterness at heart, could not forego the promptings of her genial nature, to receive the strangers hospitably. She assembled her tributary Caciques, and with a large retinue of distinguished personages, went out to meet Ovando, and escorted him, in great state, to the capital town. Areyots were sung by a selected choir of young women, while others went before, bearing palms and dancing.

Ovando had been the recipient of a general outpouring of kindness, but his heart of stone was insensible to the warmer impulses of gratitude. Professing to reciprocate the kind attentions which had been bestowed upon him, Ovando arranged a great entertainment to consist of a tilting match, or joust, with reeds. The troops, both horse and foot, were beat from quarters, and stationed as if to view the exciting and martial sport. From a banquet just given him by the Queen, Ovando joined in a game of quoits with some of his officers. When the soldiers were in their preconcerted positions, the Caciques, little aware of the foul treachery about to be practised upon them, urged Ovando to have the tilt commence. Anacaona, with her dazzling daughter, Higuenamota, and female attendants, joined in the fatal impatience.

Ovando, with well feigned reluctance, abandoned his game, and advanced to a conspicuous place in the throng of his own soldiers and natives. Everybody, except the black-hearted Spaniards, were filled with innocent and unsuspecting curiosity.

Ovando gave the signal, which was arranged to unbolt the prison doors of restraint. The blasts of trumpets rang over the multitude. The dastardly work commenced. The Caciques were seized and bound. Some were put to the torture; in their agony was wrung from them the only foundation for the foolish suspicions of Ovando, that the Queen contemplated treachery. The work of blood that ensued was too frightful to contemplate. The defenceless natives were ridden down, or hacked to pieces by the blades of Spanish swords. Eighty-four Caciques were burned at the stake or hanged. Eighty attendants, in queenly state, assembled about the person of Anacaona, were also put to the sword. What a scene for her pure eyes! What an overwhelming grief for her tender heart! At last her fearful forebodings had been realized. It was a terrible visitation. Anacaona was spared, only to be borne by her infamous and triumphant persecutors, in chains to Ovando's capital. Here a mockery of a trial was instituted. It was absurdly charged that she had plotted massacre, of whom? Nearly four hundred Spanish soldiers! This was so completely untenable, that it was tried to impeach her character; but this failed. But the scene of infamy must be crowned. The charming and good Anacaona was found guilty, in name, if not in fact, and was ignominiously hanged.

The death of the Queen was followed by the most revolting scenes of atrocity and hot-breathed persecution. All the hell-devised ingenuity of the conquerors followed those that were left; and for six months, the mountain and the forest rang with the melancholy moans of the fugitive, or expiring subjects, of the vanished dominion of Anacaona. In commemoration of the accomplishment of a deed of piety and patriotism so honorable, Ovando founded a town, which he called Santa Maria de la Verdadera Paz, (St. Mary, of the True Peace.)

CHAPTER XXXI.

HISTORY.

IT is not within the compass of my task to give a detailed history of San Domingo, yet a few of the leading events which led to certain results may not be unimportant, nor lack usefulness. The historic record of the island is filled with many stirring and sanguinary scenes, yet produced, not by causes exclusively her own, but by the mismanagement and tyranny of the parent State. The division of the island, also, between two powers, both utterly incompetent to assume the responsibility of a successful colonization, gave frequent occasion for the wars of rivalry and conquest which followed. As will be seen, the more populous and disorderly French portion in the west, led in these conflicts, and not content with the constant disruption of its own political and social fabric, launched its hostility upon the weak and unoffending Dominicans of the east. The repeated alternation of dominion between France and Spain was another cause of incessant agitation. Both sides were oppressors, and between them the prospects of the whole island were completely ruined.

In December, 1492, Columbus discovered the western portion of the island. On his return, he coasted along its entire length. So much beauty of landscape and indisputable adaptation to the purposes of settlement, determined him to plant a colony at once. Before leaving, on his homeward voyage, the colors of Castile and Leon waved over the fortress of La Navidad. Upon returning to the island and finding his little settlement wiped out, a new fortress and town were built, and called Isabella. From that time forth the possession of the island passed from its original owners into the hands of strangers.

The aboriginal population was very great, and, with proper treatment, might have been made available, but Spanish intolerance very soon inaugurated a policy of the most harsh and exacting cruelty. The natives were reduced to bondage, made doubly burdensome and hopeless, by severe measures, employed to compel the unfortunate victims to labor. The natives were an indolent race. Luxuriant and bountiful nature supplied them with the means of gratifying all their wants. There was no occasion for toil. It was natural, therefore, that every kind of extra physical exertion should be irksome. The impetuous Spaniard was determined that the natives should submit to his demands, and all attempts at opposition was attended with the most summary and desperate punishment. To what extent this bloodthirsty policy was pursued, may be judged from the melancholy fate which attended the aboriginal race of the island. Three million men, women, and children were blotted from existence by the relentless taskmasters.

The inconsiderate conduct of the Spaniards soon necessitated the introduction of a new set of laborers. As early as 1512, the first slaves were brought from Guinea, and landed on the island. This was the result of a vein of humanity, which took possession of the mother Government, and was designed as a relief to the Indians, whose numbers had already been reduced most fearfully. Hardly had ten years elapsed, than the African slaves revolted. Their numbers being small, the revolt was speedily quelled.

After a varied experience, of little more than a century, under Spanish domination, we find a new scene open.

In 1630, a party of English filibusters and French buccaneers established themselves on the north coast. In 1655, the island was invaded by the English, who landed a force of eight thousand men, at the bay of Najays, a short distance west of the capital. The English forces were commanded by Vice Admiral Penn, the father of the celebrated founder of Pennsylvania. After severe fighting, the invaders were driven off, with the loss of over three thousand men, eleven flags, and a large quantity of munitions of war. The English then withdrew to Jamaica.

In 1665, the buccaneers transferred their headquarters to the island of Tortuga. From this place they made frequent descents upon the Haytien coast, capturing cattle, and gathering supplies. The natives, on occasions of this predatory nature, generally abandoned their homes, and fled to the mountains. Sometimes, however, severe conflicts ensued. With this stolen property the invaders kept up a lively commerce with the Dutch, French, and English. A few years after, the buccaneers permanently possessed themselves of the west end of the island. This settlement, ultimately, gave France her authority to a part of Hayti.

Forty-seven years later, as the result of their triumphs over Spain, the French took possession of the whole island, and in 1697, by the treaty of Ryswick, the western portion was formally surrendered by Spain. Though Spain held an outward show of sway in the east, her authority was but nominal. French influence was, unquestionably, in the ascendancy; and, appreciating the vast resources and beauty of the island, as compared with her sisters in the Gulf of Mexico and the Caribean Sea, called her "La Reine des Antilles." In 1722, the French removed the harsh restrictions against trade and commerce. From that moment, their part of the island began to prosper.

In 1776, the courts of Versailles and Madrid determined, finally, the knotty question of a boundary by an agreement called "*Traite des Limites.*" The line was fixed at Anse à Petres, in the south, and in the bay of Manzanillo, in the north. Between these two points an imaginary line was drawn, passing through Vallier, San Raphael, the Black Mountain, and the Salt Lake. By this arrangement, the Spaniards retained possession of about two-thirds of the island; the French took one-third. The French part, however, had, at least, five times the population.

After three centuries, San Domingo was of no further use to Spain as a colony. Internal disorders and bad laws had produced the natural political distempers. The whole state was diseased, and towards the mother country all sentiments of allegiance were rapidly vanishing. The island had passed through the first century of her career, under the strangers, by the assistance of the imported labor of negroes. Their suicidal policy now gave trade a blow, by a decree of 1606, suspending all the ports of the north, and, by that means, destroying a large source of wealth. It is said that, at one time, the poverty of the people had gone to such a point, that "the greatest festival in San Domingo, was the arrival of the money to pay the administration." The revenues of the island were all but extinguished.

At the time of the outbreak of the revolution of 1789 in France, the Haytien or French portion of San Domingo was in a most prosperous condition. Under the judicious policy inaugurated in 1722, industry and capital found an abundance of employment and lucrative returns. Commerce and agriculture united in profitable unison. The ports of Hayti were crowded with shipping, and her fertile mountains and valleys were covered with plantations. Her people were growing rich, and everything promised an extraordinary prosperity. The agitations at home, however, put a sudden check to all these high anticipations.

The population of Hayti was classified under three elements. The whites, the colored, and the blacks. Amongst these three races there was an instinctive feeling of jealousy, and it was only for want of an incentive, that trouble had not long ago sprung up. The whites were the ruling class; the colored were held in rigid subserviency, while the blacks were in absolute and irremediable degradation.

In December, 1791, the memorable decree of the National Convention of France, giving to the people of color all the franchises enjoyed by French citizens, ignited the combustible material that had already been prepared. The white colonists at once took their affairs in their own hands. The authority of the home Government was entirely disregarded. A new assembly, known as the General Assembly of the French part of San Domingo, was elected, and met on the ninth of August, 1791. This action alarmed the middle race, or mulattoes, still more. They saw their only safety lay in opposition, and, accordingly, began to arm and organize in bodies. At this juncture, a new feature enters into the complications which already existed. On the twenty-third of August, in the same year, the negro slaves in the vicinity of Cape Town, rose in revolt against the French.

CHAPTER XXXII.

HISTORY—CONTINUED.

ALTHOUGH great uneasiness had been hitherto displayed, this was the opening of the dreadful and ferocious scenes which followed in rapid succession. The greatest consternation prevailed everywhere. Within two months after the contest began, it is said that over two thousand whites were massacred, and nearly two hundred sugar plantations were destroyed. In this incipient struggle ten thousand blacks perished.

The blacks and the colored race, now united against the whites, and soon secured a compulsory treaty, granting privileges to the free people of color. Unfortunately, at this juncture, the National Assembly in France receded from their action. This ignited the conflagration afresh. The struggle largely increased in dimensions, and was carried on with the most diabolical ferocity.

In hopes of correcting the fatal error which they had made, three commissioners were sent out from France, invested with competent powers to effect a settlement. Their mission was a failure. A new attempt was now made, by sending out another set of commissioners, backed by eight thousand troops. The measures adopted, in this effort to quell the rising opposition, was of the most arbitrary character. By 1793, all outward antagonism to French authority had subsided, but the conflict was by no means ended. The military force of the island consisted of fifteen thousand effective troops. In addition to this there was an available force of twenty-five thousand troops. In the mountains one hundred thousand blacks had taken refuge, and in the northern district, forty thousand slaves were still in armed hostility. In September, of the same year, a British force took possession, but was soon compelled to evacuate.

In 1794, in order to quiet the negro element, or rather to win it over, the French Directory recognized Toussaint l'Ouverture as general-in-chief of the negro armies. In the following year, by treaty, Spain ceded her portion of the island to France. The contest was unabated, and, through various bloody disorders, the affairs of San Domingo continued in the hands of the French, until 1801, when Toussaint l'Ouverture proclaimed and established an independent negro republic on the island. Bonaparte, then Chief Consul of France, not to be thus overcome, renewed his efforts to maintain his hold upon San Domingo. He sent twenty-six ships of the line, and twenty-five thousand veteran French troops, under his brother-in-law, Le Clerc. The flames of war and devastation now burst forth with increased fury. The impetuosity and vigor which characterized the inauguration of the new conflict gave the French the ascendency. They swept down all opposition. The black armies of San Domingo fell to pieces, their parts finding refuge and security alone in the mountains. Toussaint, undaunted at witnessing his crumbling fortunes, gathered about him his most devoted supporters. At an unexpected moment he appeared from the fastnesses, in which he had himself taken refuge, for a breathing spell, and fell upon the French. His standards once more floated in triumph. The French were driven back and closely pressed. Toussaint now had the affairs of the island his own way. The war had already lasted a year. He felt the suffering which had been brought upon his people by the contest. Tempted by the promises of the representatives of France, he consented to a suspension of arms. On May 7, 1803, he formally surrendered to the authority of France.

A year later, Toussaint had the bitter experience of realizing the true nature of the professions of the French. When least conscious of a cowardly plot against him, he was seized, and as a prisoner, was sent to France. Here he was at once thrown into a dark and damp dungeon, in the isolated castle of Joux, in the Jura Mountains. Having gone on a tour to Neuf Chatel, carrying the keys of the dungeon with him, the commandant was relieved, upon his return, to find that his prisoner was no more. Treachery first, and starvation at last, had accomplished what the arms of France were unable to do, to conquer the negro chieftain.

Toussaint l'Ouverture expired in April, 1803. He was one of the most extraordinary men of his day. He displayed a degree of military and political sagacity which placed him above all of his competitors in the struggles against the French in San Domingo, and made him the equal of the most notable of the world's great men. According to his biographers, he was the grandson of an African king. The larger portion of his life he passed in slavery. After passing through the various grades of promotion, from a soldier to a civil ruler and military leader, he fell, because he yielded to the noblest of human instincts —a desire to save his people through the less destructive policy of negotiation.

The seizure and incarceration of Toussaint, instead of being a death blow to all future opposition, only kindled once more the implacable hostility of the people. The blacks, outraged at the treatment which their chieftain had received, were more resolute than ever. Less than a year after the death of Toussaint a new insurrection broke out, and found capable leaders in Dessalines, Christophe, and Clerveaux. The fate of Toussaint increased, if possible, the atrocity which attended the conflict. The French, unable to withstand the opposition, November 30, 1803, agreed to evacuate the island. The ascendancy of the black element was consummated by hoisting the standard of the opposition at Cape François. On March 29, 1804, Dessalines characterized his ascent to the throne of power, by proclaiming a general massacre of the whites. In the same year a formal declaration of independence was promulgated. Dessalines followed up his triumph by having himself made Governor General for life. Not satisfied with his elevation and titles, on October 8, 1804, surrounded by great pomp and ceremony, he was crowned Emperor, under the name of Jacques

First. In 1805, the new Emperor invaded San Domingo with twenty-two thousand men. He succeeded so far as to lay siege to the capital. After a series of obstinate struggles with the Dominicans, he was compelled to decamp. He thence moved with fire and sword towards the north, and laid waste some of the most beautiful sections of the island.

The administration of imperial functions by Jacques I, was attended by a train of unheard-of barbarities. He lost even the faculty of distinguishing between his friends and his enemies. After a brief sway of two years, on October 17, 1806, Jacques I, Emperor of San Domingo, was cut short in his career by the hand of an assassin.

After a violent contention over the carcass of the State, Henry Christophe, a colored man, succeeded in being made President, in February, 1807. A few years later, aspiring to imperial honors, like his predecessor, Dessalines, Christophe was crowned Emperor, under the name of Henry I. At the same time Pelhion exercised Presidential authority at Port-au-Prince.

In 1808, General Ferrand was the French Governor of the Spanish post. In that year, Don Juan Sanchez Ramirez, of Cotuy, headed a rebellion against the French. The following year, with an army of Dominican herdsmen, he encountered the French forces near Seybo, at a place called Palo-Hincado. The French were completely routed, and Ferrand, unequal to the misfortune, committed suicide. July 11, 1809, Don Juan Sanchez, with his army, entered the capital and threw the Spanish flag to the breeze.

In 1814, by the treaty of Paris, France relinquished her right, to the eastern part of the island, to Spain. This once more divided the contest.

Pethion held on in the western department, and only succumbed to the indisputable argument of a natural death. Juan Pedro Boyer was elected as his successor, in May, 1818.

In October, 1818, the Emperor Christophe, growing tired of his exalted station, and particularly verifying, in his own experience, the disquiet surrounding the head of a king, disposed of his authority, and all future doubts, by committing suicide. One month after Christophe's voluntary and mechanical abdication of his office and life, the western end of the island became an unit, under Boyer, as Regent for life.

In November, 1821, the Spanish Governor of the East was seized by a party of insurgents, headed by a lawyer, named José Nunez Cáceres. A declaration of independence was issued, which, being supported by armed force, resulted, in the following year, in wiping out once more the authority of Spain. A party sprung up in favor of union with the black Republic of the West. The popular tide, with some coercion, following in the same direction, the union of the two sections was consummated, January 21, 1822, by unfurling the Haytien flag from the walls of San Domingo city. On the ninth of the following month the keys of the city were handed over to President Boyer, in person. He entered at once, and took possession. In 1825, France recognized the united State, in consideration of liberal commercial privileges.

Now followed a period of long quiet. Under Boyer's rule, the resources of the island once more looked up. But after a successful rule of eighteen years, Boyer experienced the instability of his position by being deposed.

In August, 1849, Hayti, or the West, proclaimed an Empire, under Solouque, as Faustin I. Three years after, that aspiring individual was crowned. In December, 1858, Geffard was proclaimed President of the Republic of Hayti. The next year Faustin First abdicated. In September, 1865, Geffard himself was compelled to resign. The last act in the scene is the execution of Salnave, and the establishment of Saget in power.

We will now turn to the East. For twenty-two years the Spanish portion of the island was held in subjection to the Government of Hayti. On the twenty-seventh day of February, 1844, the citizens of the city of San Domingo, under Juan Pablo Duarte, rose, and, overcoming the Haytien garrison, declared their liberty, under the name of the Dominican Republic, with the motto, *Dios, Patria and Libertad,* (God, our Country, and Liberty.) After a brief struggle, they succeeded in throwing off the yoke of their black neighbors. The Haytiens continued for a short time to hold the districts of Cabas, Hincha, Bánica, San Miguel de la Atalaya, and San Rafael de la Augusturo, but finally withdrew within their own borders. Great Britain and France, a few years after, recognized the existence of the new State, and were followed by other Powers.

The affairs of San Domingo were kept in incessant disturbance by invasions from Hayti. The Dominicans invariably met these depredations with patriotic zeal, and hurled the arms of the black emperors back within the limits of their own territory.

General Santana, afterwards called "*Libertador de la Patria,*" was chosen first President, and had

Buenaventura Baez, the present President, as his friend and adviser.

In 1849, when Santana declined to accept a reelection, Baez was made President, as the next most worthy person in the Republic. This gentleman was born at Ozua, one of the chief towns of San Domingo. From his earliest childhood he took great interest in the politics of his country. He had also before him the deeds and worth of his father, who took a leading part in the revolution of 1808. The father was a man of means, and, therefore, well educated his children. Buenaventura Baez had five brothers, two of whom, as well as Baez himself, were educated in Paris. Upon entering the arena of politics, the brothers at once espoused the cause of Buenaventura, and, at different times, have held offices of trust and influence.

The President first brought himself into notice by the conspicuous part he took in the Constitutional Assembly of '44, and is said to be the father of the constitution.

As soon as Baez secured the succession to Santana, the friendship, which had hitherto existed between the two men, broke into a bitter rivalry. Baez ruled the country from 1849 till 1853. In the latter year, Santana again came in, and as the first act of his administration, banished Baez from the island. Baez went to New York, and remained there, taking an active part in all the hostile movements against his rival. In 1857, Baez was again called in, and the next year Santana once more headed a rising which compelled Baez to flight. Since the independence of 1844, until the transfer to Spain, Santana and Baez alternated in power, with the exception of a brief interruption of about four months by Jimenez.

In March, 1861, a movement in favor of annexation to Spain was started. So unprepared were the people, generally, to make any opposition, that by the 20th of the following May, the island was once more united to the fortunes of the old monarchy. Hostility to Spain was part of the nature of a Dominican. Barely had a month passed when the dissatisfaction of the people began to show itself in Moca and Cercado de los Matas. The first regular blow was struck at Capotilla, on the 18th of August, 1863. By November, the revolutionists had possession of nearly the entire island. Spain declared all the ports in a state of blockade. At length the opposition became so formidable, that Spain could no longer hold out. On July 11, 1565, the Spanish flag was again hauled down. The Spaniards were in hopes of still keeping Samana bay, but twelve days after were compelled to withdraw from there also. This restored to the Dominican Republic its full sway upon every foot of Dominican soil. The restored Government was very soon recognized by the great powers.

After the driving out of the Spaniards for the second time, José Maria Cabral came into power as President. It was complained, by his friends, that his administration was too much influenced by leniency and toleration. By others it was asserted that he was a man of good heart, but lacked force of character.

In October, 1866, forty men from Curaçoa, a Dutch island off the Spanish Main, landed on the southern coast of San Domingo, in the district of Higuey, about one hundred miles east of the city of San Domingo. These men were in the interest of Buenaventura Baez, who was living at Curaçoa. The entire party was captured and sentenced to be shot, but the penalty was commuted.

In July, of the following year, a number of Baezistas, led by a brother of Baez, landed from a Danish schooner, at Monte Christi, but not meeting with response retreated.

These movements led to the breaking off of relations between Hayti and San Domingo, by Cabral, upon the grounds of the former government furnishing aid to Baez.

In January, 1868, the political situation became more than ever complicated. The country had now risen against the government; but Cabral still held the capital. The leading cause of this sudden change was the worthlessness of the paper money which had been issued by the government, and was now valued at four hundred dollars paper for one dollar gold.

Before the middle of January, affairs assumed so serious an aspect that the troops were withdrawn from the country, and stationed within the walls of the capital. Shots were exchanged with the country people and a small force outside. General José Hungria had already established a provisional government at Santiago de los Caballeros.

On January 31, the capital of the Republic, being closely invested, was compelled to surrender to Hungria. Cabral and Pimental, with about one hundred men, embarked for Porto Cabello, in Venezuela. In February, a triumvirate was established for the government of the island, consisting of Generals José Hungra, Gomez, and Luciano. On the twenty-ninth of March following Baez arrived at San Domingo. He was enthusiastically received by the populace. In some parts he was proclaimed dictator, but these powers he declined. On the second of May, 1868, Baez was installed President of the Dominican Republic. The constitution of 1854 was adopted, with some amendments. The paper money was taken up at four hundred dollars for one dollar.

Since the inauguration of Baez that gentleman has remained in power, and has exercised in many respects a liberal policy, and has made concessions looking to a development of the resources of the island.

Almost immediately after his deposition, and flight from the country, Cabral returned and inaugurated a movement, having in view his own reinstatement. Establishing himself in the mountains, on the Haytien frontiers, Cabral received assistance from the Cacos, or Haytien rebels, who had taken refuge there, and also from malcontents of San Domingo. With various fortunes, and remarkable persistency, Cabral kept up a desultory warfare, much to the annoyance of Baez, and injury to the welfare of the island.

Such was the condition of things in July, 1869.

CHAPTER XXXIII.

TOPOGRAPHY—MOUNTAINS—VALLEYS—BAYS—
MINERAL WEALTH.

THE island of San Domingo, (Häiti, Hayti, Hispaniola,) lying between the eighteenth and twentieth parallels of north latitude, and from three to nine degrees east of Washington, is divided into two independent political divisions, the Dominican and Haytien Republics. The former, lying on the east, occupies about three-fifths of the entire island, and has an area of about 17,500 square miles. The surface of this portion possesses a diversity of elevation, from rolling savannas to lofty mountains. The mountain system consists of two principal ranges, the northern following the trend, and close to the northern coast; the southern ranging, in general direction, from east to west, and about ten leagues inland from the southern coast. These ranges are classified into ten principal groups of mountains. First, the mountains of Samana, extending from the east to the west of the peninsula of the same name, with the peaks of Diablo and Pilon de Azucar. Second, the mountains of Macorio, extending seventy-five miles from east to northwest, with the distinctive peaks of Quita, Espuela, and Cucurucho. Third, the mountains of Monte Christi, ranging from east to northwest, one hundred and twenty miles from the top of Sella de Caballo, (Horse's Saddle,) with the principal peaks of Nord Pico, (3,000 feet,) Diego Campo, near Santiago de los Caballeros, (3,600 feet,) Santa Anna, (3,000 feet,) and Muraco, (3,000 feet.) Fourth, Sierra del Cibao, on the north side, extending seventy-eight miles from east to west. Fifth, the mountains of Constanza, extending from east to west one hundred and twenty miles, with the high peaks of Entre los Rios (6,700 feet) and group, Pico de Yacki, (6,000 feet,)—north of these, extend several beautiful small spurs. Sixth, the mountains of San Rafael, which unite, on the west, with Monte Negros and the Lomas de Cahos, one hundred and sixty-eight miles in length. Seventh, Sierras de la Hilera, (central,) stretching three hundred miles, east and west, from Sierra Gorda to the river Neiba—(the peak of the range, Loma Zina, is 9,300 feet high.) Eighth, the group of Serramas de Jaina, Nizao, Bani, and Azua, seventy-five miles. Ninth, Sierras of Neiba, seventy-seven miles in length; with its highest peak, Lomade Panza, 5,500 feet. Tenth, Las Sierras de Manuel and Barbaruco, extending seventy-eight miles from east to west.

Between these mountain groups, covered with profuse vegetation to their very summits, lie valleys of unexampled fertility, as follows:

The valley of the Neiba, the westernmost, lies along the southern slope, and contains about seven hundred square miles. The Neiba river and a range of mountains separate it, on the east, from the plains of Azua and Bani, and, to the west, it is bounded by the river of Dames and the lake of Henriquilla. The valley of Azua, covering an area of 1,300 square miles, possesses a soil of extraordinary richness. West of the capital, San Domingo city, is the rich valley of Bani, extending from the Nisao river to Ocoa. This section is admirably adapted to pasturage, as are, also, the fine arable lands near the port of Palanque, and the Savanna Grande, at the outlet of the Wasao.

To the east of the capital, are the immense meadows called Los Llanos, or the Plains, extending from the Ozama river to the easternmost point of the island. In early times, the Spaniards possessed extensive sugar plantations here—to-day, only a few cattle are to be seen.

The great valley, surpassing all others in fertility, is the La Vega Real, or the Royal Meadow. It lies in the centre of the island, between the two chains of mountains, and is watered by numerous streams, which form the Yaque and Yuna—the one emptying into the bay of Manzanilla, in the northwest, and the other, into the bay of Samana, on the east. This stretch of open country is two hundred and forty miles in length, and from thirty to forty miles in width. This valley is the garden-spot of the island, and possesses a climate of great health and salubrity.

The extreme length of San Domingo is four hundred miles, and its widest point, in a straight line, one hundred and fifty miles.

San Domingo also possesses a large number of ports and anchorages available to commerce. Those to the north of Punta Engaño are Cabeza de Toro, Babaro los Ranchito, Arena Gorda, Macao, and Port Jicaco, or English Harbor, (Puerto de los Ingleses.) During the summer months, when the trade winds culty; but during the winter season this part of the coast is extremely dangerous. Next comes the great bay of Samana. The bays and beaches, commencing at Cape Samana northward, are Las Galeras, Rincon, Puerto Escondido, Boca de San Juan, Hermitans, Limon, Punta de los Pescadores, Boca del Estillero, and de Laberiana and Punta de Moretes. On the north coast from Samana, towards Puerto Plata, are Matanzas, Cabaret, Sousa, Breganlin, and the narrow harbor of Puerto Plata itself. Between Puerto Plata and Punta Isabella are Soufle and Puerto Caballo. Next, Jacaquito and Monte Christi. The last, on the north coast, is the fine bay of Manzanilla. Formerly, the Rio Yaque, called by Columbus Rio de Oro, emptied into the bay of Monte Christi, but, at the beginning of the present century, it changed its course into the bay of Manzanilla. The latter is second only to Samana, and has all the facilities of harboring an extensive commerce. It is protected by Cays, called the Seven Brothers. It receives the Yaque, on the eastern part, and the Massacre, or Dajabon, river on the south. The bay has from seven to ten fathoms water. The proximity of the bay to the Haytien border, the Dajabon formerly being acknowledged as the boundary between the Spanish and French parts, and being still so claimed by the Dominican Government, and as well, in connection with the troubles often arising between the two sections, has been almost entirely abandoned. The rest of the inlets, estuaries, and bays, available to ocean vessels, are the Ozama, at San Domingo City, Chaldera, Ocoa, Barahona, to the west, and Cumayasa and Rouman, to the east.

Of the mineral wealth of the island little can be said, as no thoroughly scientific investigation has ever been made.

There are certainly very flattering indications of gold and other valuable metals; but as yet it is mere speculation as to the quantities. A geologist has been appointed, and surveys were being made at the time of my visit.

According to various authorities, there is no doubt respecting the existence of gold, copper, and iron. A vein of silver, with lead, is reported as having been discovered about twenty years ago, by an Englishman named Henneke.

The distribution of valuable metals and precious stones in the island, according to the traces which have been found, may be set down as more particularly belonging to the following localities: Gold in the ranges of the Cibao, the Verdé, Yaque, and section, history tells us, led to the foundation of Cotuy, La Vega, Santiago, Guaba, and other points. Silver in Jarabacoa; copper in San Christobal, and the vicinity of Santiago and Cotuy; iron in the mountains of Prieta, north of San Domingo, Cotuy, and other points; cinnabar in the provinces of Santiago and Christobal; tin in the province of Seibo and district of Higuey; sulphur at various points, but particularly in the mountains of Biajama; limestone, marble, alabaster, and jasper of all colors; porphyry and talc in the communes of Bani, Aqua, Seibo, and Santiago; emeralds in the mountains near Cotuy; rock salt in great abundance in the province of Neiba; rock crystal and coal on the peninsula of Samana.

There is no doubt that the geologist and mineralogist would find in San Domingo a fine field of study and exploration. But, whatever may be said of her undeveloped mineral resources, it is certain the greatest and surest wealth of San Domingo is in her fertile soil, her valuable forests, her beautiful rivers. The various productions, finding upon her mountain sides and rolling savannas, a congenial soil, properly cultivated, and with population to increase the area adapted to the industry of man, would prove more valuable than all the mines of the Hayna and the Cibao.

CHAPTER XXXIV.

PRODUCTIONS—WOODS—DYE-STUFFS—FRUITS.

T is natural to suppose that such a diversity of surface and fertile soil is adapted to a great variety of vegetable productions. Immense forests of mahogany are found in all parts of the island, that of the south side, however, being considered the best. The cutting and shipping of this valuable wood employs about one-fifth of the people of the country. The supply would seem inexhaustible, there being numerous forests that have never been touched. The capa tree, resembling white oak, is found in great abundance in the southern and eastern portions of the island. It is smaller and more crooked than the oak, and bears about the same relation to it as does the live, to the pasture oak, of the United States. The espanillo, or satinwood, is found on the south side of the island, but more rare than other cabinet woods. The San Domingo lignumvitæ is famous. Among the dyewoods are principally fustic and Campeachy, or logwood. The latter abounds most on the south side. The other trees consist of a species of oak, locust, yellow and black cedar, cerba, brazilletta, cabilma, pitch pine, marny, amendra, tamarind, mango, palm, and orange of several varieties. The palm tree is especially useful to the natives. Oil from the nuts constitutes a principal article of domestic use, while they also form food for the wild hogs, which are the principal wealth of the mountaineers. Hats, baskets, saddles, panniers, and ceroons, are made of certain portions of the leaves. This valuable tree also furnishes the weather boarding for the native houses, and near the top the external covering, called *yoguas*, is employed in thatching the houses and for other purposes.

The agricultural productions adapted to the soil and climate, are tobacco, sugar, coffee, cocoa, and cotton, and an almost endless variety of fruits. The tobacco, found in the country by Columbus, was of a very superior quality, and the cultivated plant of to-day is justly celebrated. The best quality is raised on the great plain of Cotuy and Le Vega, and taken to Santiago for sale, and thence across the mountains of Cibao, for shipment at Porto Plata. The cultivation of sugar almost disappeared after the departure of the Spaniards. The few proprietors in the vicinity of San Christobal, Palenque, Azua, and Maniel, who shipped their crops to San Domingo City, raised in the year 1862, 3,000 ceroons, at a cost of two cents per pound, on the estates. The growth of this staple has much increased within the past few years, but is almost entirely consumed in the country in the manufacture of rum and molasses, or eaten in the cane.

The growth of coffee is insufficient to meet the wants of the population, but in connection with cocoa has proved very successful. In the country, I observed at places, numerous coffee trees, apparently growing wild, but in reality some hardier plants, that had withstood the opposition of the rank vegetation which now covers the old Spanish plantations.

Cotton grows spontaneously on a small tree. The trees average from 150 to 200 bolls, and grow on the poorest soil and in the crevices of the rocks. I have seen it thriving in the rubbish of ruined cities. In the time of Columbus cotton yarn was manufactured in great abundance, and the natives (Indians) would exchange large balls of twenty-five pounds weight for pieces of broken glass. Columbus, by way of a tax, compelled each individual to furnish an arroba of twenty-five pounds every three months.

The gum of the lignumvitæ, known as the gum guiac, is also an important item of industry. The raising of bees, and the production of honey and beeswax, occupies much attention, and meets with great success. The annatto plant, which produces a fine dyestuff called by the French rocon, grows finely. Indigo, formerly cultivated in large quantities, and exported to Spain, is now only known as a weed troubling the planters.

Upon San Domingo nature has also bestowed her bounty with a lavish hand. The native, unused or loth to toil, finds ample and spontaneous food awaiting him in forest and grove. In the quality, quantity, and variety of her fruits, no island in the world surpasses San Domingo.

The most important productions, as an article of food, is the plantain, and next to it, the banana. Both grow in great abundance. The former, which is considered a vegetable, is a most important article of diet. It is always found upon the tables of the rich, or upon the rude spread of the poor. It is prepared in several ways—baked, boiled, or cut in slices and fried. There are several varieties of both species. In the banana, the manzana, or apple banana, is the larger fruit, though the fig banana is more delicate and delicious. The plantain blossoms in beautiful flower cones of purple. All the year round the clusters of ripening or ripened fruit may be seen.

Next to the plantain and banana, in its use to man, is the cocoa-nut. This prodigious and fruitful plant thrives remarkably. In a year a single tree, in a suitable soil and situation, it is said, will drop as high as two hundred nuts, while in poorer places the yield is but forty nuts for the same time. The usual time for the tree to arrive at maturity, I was informed, was expedited to five years, by throwing several times a year a small quantity of salt into the heart of the plume of the branches. The fruit is applied to a number of uses. The edible part is a pleasant article of diet, the milk is drank, or employed in cooking. The oil, manufactured from the meat, has medicinal virtues for bruises, rheumatic fevers, and is even said to be invaluable for pulmonary troubles. The oil, also, enters into several domestic uses, and as well as an article of commerce. The hard shell forms cups and saucers. The wood of the tree is used in building, and the leaves answer a diversity of purposes, in making *macutas*,

The bread of the country is made out of the bulbous root of the *yuca*. In this form it is known as cassava, an article of diet handed down from the aboriginal inhabitants of the country. The *yuca* is ground and mixed with cocoa-nut milk, after which it is laid out in immense thin cakes, and, in the primitive style of the earliest occupants of the country, is baked, by folding the cake in banana leaves, and placing it near the fire. The *arapa*, a sort of hoecake, made out of new corn, is also very extensively used, and is not unpleasant to the palate. This is made by taking the young corn, cleaned from the cob, and mixing it with an equal quantity of cocoa-nut, grated. The whole is mixed with cocoa-nut milk, and baked the same as cassava. There is no difficulty in keeping up a constant succession of yuca and corn all the year round. The *yantilla*, generally found wild, has a root which takes the place of plantains, yuca, and yams, in times of scarcity.

Of the fruits there is the *mango*, a beautiful tree. It yields at the age of four years, and in the months of May and June. The *ciamete* is a round, green pulpy fruit, which comes in about February, and runs into March. The *guava* is a willing bearer all the year. The *guanabana*, the fruit of which is often called "consolidated lemonade," on account of its cooling acidulous taste, pays its contribution to the appetite of man during the months of February and March, and ceases in April, and blossoms again, and sends for another crop in midsummer. The best varieties of oranges appear from September to May, but some species of the fruit are to be had during the entire year. We also find the delicious sub-acid pomegranate, the creamy custard apples, tamarinds, wild plums, pine apples, limes, in their appropriate seasons.

The ginger and arrow-root thrive remarkably, and in addition to their medicinal uses, their long, sparkling green leaves, very much resembling a garden lily, make a beautiful border for walks. A delightful wine, much used on the island, is also made out of these roots. Limes make, also, a pleasant beverage.

The *calabaza*, a sort of tropical pumpkin, or gourd, is much grown, on account of the convenient vessels, for domestic uses, made out of the fruit.

Of the vegetables which thrive best on the island, are the asparagus, beans, tomatoes, ocra, egg-plant, and peppers, which are fit for use in May, and green corn, cabbage, sweet potatoes, and parsnips, later.

tudes, when nature, having accomplished her annual bearing, lies idle, the farmer in San Domingo experiences a busy season in putting in his corn, cotton, and sugar. Indeed, the entire year has its appropriate duties to be performed, in preparing the soil and depositing the seed in the ground, and has its never-ending maturity of fruits and crops. The rapidity of growth of all vegetation is amazing. Every month has its returns and its beauty. The season of roses begins in February, and lasts in endless profusion for five months. March is the choice month for fruits and flowers. In April, all the vegetables of New York in June, are ready for the table. In May, the tamarind, the wild plum, the pomegranate, the *guava*, and coffee, are in blossom. The custard apples and *guanabana*, come between the *caimete*, in February and March, and the *mango* in June and July, Corn, planted in February and March, is ready in September. The *yuca* requires from six to eight months, and the enormous roots of the yam from eight to ten months. It is a singular fact that plants, put out in October and November, have less foliage, and are slower to mature, than those planted in summer.

The staple productions of the island, distributed by districts, are:

San Domingo: Mahogany, lignum vitæ, dye-woods, wax, hides, and sugar.

Azua: Mahogany, a little sugar. The district of San Juan, in this province, is famous for its grazing, and raises large numbers of horses and cattle. Hides are here a leading article of export.

Seybo: In this province, the principal source of revenue, is cattle-raising, though considerable quantities of mahogany are also cut.

La Vega and Santiago are devoted chiefly to tobacco-raising. These two districts are known under the general name, "El Cibao," and constitute the most populous portions of the Republic. The people, also, are particularly noted for their industry.

It is a remarkable fact that San Domingo has no wild animals. It is true, a few hogs were in the forests, without owners, but can hardly be classed under that head. Nor are any snakes known to exist, save a species similar to, and as harmless as, the garter-snake. Scorpions, tarantulas, and centipedes, are occasionally met with in the forest.

CHAPTER XXXV.

CLIMATE—FEVERS—TEMPERATURE—SEASONS—POPULATION—THE PEOPLE—THEIR HABITS.

THE climate of San Domingo is better than that of any other of the islands of the Antilles. The country being high, no miasmatic vapors spread over the land to generate epidemics.

The strangers' fever, as it is called, is a mild type of the fever and ague of the United States. The *calentura* is a broken condition of the system, induced, it is said, by miasma arising from the rank vegetation of the forests. It assumes every type, from a simple chill and fever to the most complicated typhoidal form. In the less serious cases, the usual *tisana* is given. The fever runs about nine days, during which time the victim should discard heavy food. The symptoms are dizziness, and excessive pains in the limbs.

In cases of fevers, a warm *tisana* of green limes is used to drive out the chills. This is prepared by cutting up from six to eight limes in a small vessel of boiling water, and should be taken sweetened.

The cholera has visited the island but twice, and then in time of war, and was brought there by foreign enemies. During my stay in the city, I heard of but one death, and no serious cases of sickness.

The year, in San Domingo, is divided into two seasons—the wet and the dry. The latter is said to commence in December, though I was informed by the residents that January was really the first month of the season. By February, the rains suspend almost entirely, when a period of dry weather, for about two months, ensues. From May to October, is a season of almost daily rains. There are, also, what are called the spring and fall rains. The rains fall, almost invariably, in the afternoon.

The temperature of the island is no hotter, and certainly is more grateful, than that of New York during the summer. The alternation of land and sea-breezes daily ventilate the atmosphere. The best season on the island is during the months of January, February, and March. The air is then salubrious and healthy. For invalids, unable to withstand the rigor of the northern winter, it affords a delightful relief.

Owing to the oppressive and suicidal policy of

Spain, and, subsequently, the incessant political disorders which disturbed the peace and development of the country, the population of San Domingo is very small. It is said, by contemporary authorities, that the primitive population of the whole island was great, some estimating it as high as three millions of souls. The course pursued by the Spaniards soon wiped these innocent people from the face of the land. The importation of slaves, for a time, kept up the population, in numbers, to an average of from six to seven hundred thousand of human beings of all grades; but disease and the sword were too much, even for the combined accessions by the natural laws of increase and by importation.

The population of the Spanish part of the island in the year 1785 was estimated as follows:

Free persons, of all descriptions,	122,640
Slaves,	30,000
	152,640
At the same time the population of the French portion was,	523,803
Total,	676,443

Between the years 1791 and 1820 the endless and sanguinary wars of that period had a visible effect upon the population.

Mackenzie, in his notes on Hayti, gives the population of the Spanish part in 1824, as follows:

Arondissements.	Communes.	Population.	
Monte Christi,	Monte Christi,	1,029	
Puerto Plata,	Puerto Plata,	4,534	
Azua,	Azua,	3,208	
	Neyba,	3,516	
			6,724
San Domingo,	The city and commune,	11,205	
	Bani,	2,321	
	Seybo,	5,964	

alluded to in the tables of 1824, includes a population of about one hundred and twenty thousand souls. The foreign population does not embrace more than a few consular officers, merchants and sailors, travelers and vagabonds. The people of San Domingo are divided into three classes—the whites, mulattoes, and blacks; but the relative number of each is not know. It is certain, however, that the whites are vastly inferior in population to either of the other divisions, probably not more than one-tenth.

The character of the people, generally, is that of an easy, thoughtless, inoffensive set, who would prefer to live in listless forgetfulness of the duties or responsibilities of life. Their notions are exceedingly primitive, and their wants exceedingly few. The fashions, a year or two out of date, are adopted for occasions of ceremony. At other times, the women loll about in a loose gown. The children, boys and girls, run naked about the house, or in the streets, until they have reached the ages of at least six, and sometimes go in the same primitive Garden-of-Eden attire for several years longer.

The relations between the sexes, and between man and wife, is of an infinitely lower standard than our own. Woman is looked upon for her domestic uses solely, and not as a companion. If in comfortable circumstances, they lounge about from morning until night, in hammocks, or amuse themselves in divers ways. The poorer classes attend to their household duties.

There is no regular system of schools, by means of which the poorer classes can have the benefits of an education. The boys of the rich are generally educated abroad. At the time of my visit, I was shown through the college of San Luis Gonzega. This institution had been established two and a half centuries. I was entertained, while in the building, by the students' band, consisting of about fifteen performers, upon brass and reed instruments. The institution was under the control of priests, and was well attended. From what information I can gather in conversation, I concluded the course of instruction was very thorough. The education of women is considered a subject of little importance.

I will say, that my own treatment, while on the island, was of the most flattering and hospitable character. From the President down to the humblest *buerroquero* I met the same uniform evidences of respect, and a disposition to open to me every avenue of information. This was the case both in the cities, and towns, and in the country. I satisfied myself that the people are not instinctively vicious, but infinitely prefer to pass their days in quiet, and, as opportunity offers, their nights in festivity. The people struck me as a law-abiding class.

In point of order and morality, the city of San Domingo is a model. Its governor, Damion Baez, a brother of the President, is a man of more than ordinary executive ability. With an efficient police force at his control, the most perfect quiet constantly prevails. During the five days I remained in the city I saw not a single instance of intoxication, nor a sign of a personal rencontre. Robbery is unknown. The doors of the houses are rarely locked. The people allow their valuables to lie around with perfect indifference. The only prisoners I saw, were those confined for political offences.

A few ambitious men, as in all countries, find their followers, a worthless scape-grace set, and with these create turmoil and disorder, just sufficient to divert or destroy the growth and development of the material resources of the country.

With a strong Government, and a few severe examples, for the edification of the turbulent spirits, I feel assured there is enough virtue left in the Dominican people to make a peaceable, industrious, and enterprising race. All they need, is example.

With the influx of emigration, they would soon find themselves, not only prosperous, but worthy of higher aims in life than a mere vegetable existence.

CHAPTER XXXVI.

TRADE AND COMMERCE.

AT different times, since her discovery, the island of San Domingo has alternated between a state of great prosperity and ruinous depression. Immediately preceding the outbreak of 1789, everything was in a most flourishing condition. The wars which have since ensued, have resulted in almost destroying her. The following facts show the fall, in the brief space of thirty-five years:

1789.—Clayed sugar, 47,516.531 lbs.; Muscovado sugar, 95,573,300 lbs.; coffee, 76,835,219 lbs.; cotton, 7,004,274 lbs.; indigo, 758,628 lbs.; molasses, 25,749 hhds.

1824.—No clayed sugar; Muscovado sugar, 2,020 lbs.; coffee, 36,034,300 lbs.; cotton, 815,697 lbs.;

cocoa, 339,937 lbs.; indigo, none; molasses, none; dye-woods, 3,948,190 lbs.; tobacco, 503,425 lbs.; mahogany, 2,986,469 lbs.

To-day, there are no statistical records in the Dominican part of the island prior to 1817, all such documents having been removed to Cuba, by the Spaniards.

The imports of gold were not declared at the custom-house, and the amounts of drafts on foreign countries negotiated here, in payment for produce, amounted to four hundred thousand pounds sterling.

During my own visit to the island I experienced great difficulty in obtaining a clear statement of the trade and financial statistics of the country. No public records were kept from which a tabular list might be compiled. The only accounts were those at the custom-houses, and these were of the simplest character. From this source, with the assistance of Señor Durocher, collector of the port of San Domingo, I was enabled to gather a small amount of reliable material, from which an idea may be obtained in relation to the present commercial and financial condition of the island of San Domingo.

The four open ports at which custom-houses were established, were Puerto Plata, San Domingo City, Samana, and Azua.

The value of the imports and exports, at these ports, for the year ending June 30, 1868, was:

	Exports.	Imports.
Puerto Plata	$596,459	$354,808
San Domingo	171,379	259,501
Azua	15,000	20,000
Samana	6,000	8,000
Total	$788,838	$642,309

Excess of exports, $53,471.

In the same year the amount of tobacco shipped from Puerto Plata to Hamburg and Bremen reached 70,000 quintals, of 100 pounds each, and sugar 91,500 hogsheads. Seven American vessels arrived in port, with cargoes valued at $22,500, and carried in exports to the United States $16,625. Total imports by American and English vessels, $27,000; total exports by same, $50,700.

In regard to the commercial relations of the island, vessels of any nation have perfect right to enter any open port of the Dominican Republic with lawful merchandise. They can discharge and take in cargo, paying for all expenses one dollar and fifty cents per ton. If the vessels take in the return cargo, at one or more points on the coast, there is an extra expense of one dollar per ton, termed "coast permission."

Goods imported from the United States direct, pay twenty-five per cent., on the custom-house tariff, which is, more or less, according to United States prices.

The export duties are: On coffee and cocoa, fifty cents per hundred pounds; sugar, twelve-and-a-half cents per hundred pounds; logwood, lignumvitæ, brazilete, fustic, and any other dye-woods, one dollar per ton; tortoise shells, twenty-five cents per pound; white wax, one dollar and fifty cents per hundred pounds; yellow wax, one dollar per hundred pounds, mahogany and cedar, five dollars per thousand feet; hides, six cents each; honey, two cents per gallon; molasses, two cents per gallon; gum guaiacum, fifty cents per quintal; tobacco, fifty cents per quintal; dividivi, free.

The principal shipping of the island was direct with Europe, either in vessels arriving with cargo, and open to charter, or vessels chartered in St. Thomas, and come here to take cargo. St. Thomas was a sort of base of business operations for the whole island. A Spanish steamer, running between Havana and St. Thomas, visits San Domingo once a month, each way, for mails and passengers.

The rates of freight for Europe and the United States vary, according to circumstances. Formerly, cargoes were carried by sailing vessels, exclusively. During the year 1869, the establishment of a steam-line between the ports of San Domingo and New York has diverted much of the tobacco, which now goes by steam to New York, and is there transhipped for Havre, or Hamburg, by steam.

The principal articles of import are linens, cotton goods, a few woolens, cutlery, iron goods, wines, brandies, provisions, flour, butter, cheese, lard, candles, refined sugar, oil, and lumber. To counterbalance this trade, the island sends abroad mahogany, cabelma, an inferior quality of mahogany, satin wood and cedar wood, baria wood for masts, San Domingo oak for ship-building, lignum vitæ-fustic for dyeing, gum guaiacum, bees-wax, and honey, tortoise-shell, hides, cocoa, tobacco, sugar, and ginger. Formerly, large quantities of cotton and coffee were also shipped.

Another article of commerce is a variety of starch, prepared from the root of the plant called *guallaga*. On the southern coast, and as far as the coraline limestone formations extend, this tree is to be met with. The root contains an amylaceous, or starchy, matter, with a bitter taste. (It is said that, during the siege of the capital, in 1808–'09, the poor lived on this, but it produced a fearful mortality.) The United States furnishes the provisions, England the manufactured goods, and France the liquors.

Since the disturbances, incident to the overthrow of foreign authority, the finances of San Domingo have never been in a satisfactory or responsible condition. In 1844, when the Dominicans assumed the reins of power, a currency, issued and guarantied by the Haytien Government, was in use. This was soon called in, and exchanged for Dominican paper, and an additional issue of nearly a half million dollars was made. Various other issues have since been made, and the fluctuations between the gold standard, and the nominal value of the paper, has, at times, exhibited very extraordinary examples of the ups and downs of an irresponsible financial system, based upon an unstable Government. In the payment of local dues, the Government of late years has been in the habit of issuing orders on the custom-houses, to be paid out of the receipts. It has not been unusual to have these orders largely exceed the receipts, and at this time considerable amounts of indebtedness, in this form, is outstanding. The revenues are, almost exclusively, from duties on imports and exports. Merchants, shop-keepers, tradesmen, and the like, pay a license-fee, but there are no land or house taxes.

The coins chiefly met with on the island are the American gold dollar, eagles and double-eagles, the Spanish and South American doubloons; also the English and French gold coins. For silver, the American and Spanish coins are employed. The former are the more popular. At the custom-house, the English pound avordupois and the imperial gallon are used; in wholesale transactions, the French weight. The English yard is used by retailers.

CHAPTER XXXVII.

THE GOVERNMENT—MILITARY AND NAVAL FORCE.

THE Government of San Domingo is essentially military. Its various functions are embraced in an executive, represented by a President, and, in the event of his death, a Vice-President; the legislative, by a *Senatus Consultum* of nine members; and the judicial, by a Supreme Court, presided over by a Chief Justice. The *Senatus Consultum* combines legislative and advisory powers, and is presided over by a President chosen by itself. The President is surrounded by a Cabinet composed of a Secretary of State and Interior, a Secretary of War and Marine, a Minister of Finance; and of Public Instruction and Justice.

The territory of the Republic is divided into five provinces and two maritime districts.

Santo Domingo de Guzman, which lies on the south coast, at the mouth of the Ozama, and is the seat of Government; Compostela de Azua, and Santa Cruz del Seybo, both, also, on the southern coast; Conception de la Vega, in the interior, and Santiago de los Caballeros, on the northern coast. Puerto Plata and Samana are the maritime districts.

Each province and district is ruled over by a civil and military governor. For the convenience of local administration, each province and district is subdivided into *communes*, and communes, again, into sections.

The President is, in every respect, the head of the Republic, and in his hands rests all the power, military or civil.

The army consists of a few thousand regular troops, really nothing more than an organized mob. These are posted in small detachments in the different towns. The people, naturally, are averse to military duty, and resort to every means to avoid it. The men are armed with *machetas*, and such fire-arms as the Government may have purchased from various parties.

The uniform of the Dominican soldier consists of a straw hat, a shirt, and a pair of pantaloons. His rations are composed of beef, at intervals, a little bread, if convenient, and a liberal supply of sugar cane, distributed by the yard. At all times in the day, off duty, the Dominican soldier can be seen industriously masticating at one end of a piece of cane, while the other extremity he holds in his hand.

There is no regular military organization. Desertion is common, and is most harshly punished. In the warlike movements their tactics amount to nothing more than guerilla attacks and retreats.

The military property of the government consists of the stronghold of the city of San Domingo, which comprises within its walls sixteen forts and small redoubts, two heavy gun batteries, quarters for over ten thousand men, two magazines, together with artillery and munitions of war; the Castle of Jania, on the river of the same name; the Fort of San Louis, at Santiago de los Caballeros; the Castle of San Felipe, at Puerto Plata; the Fort of San Francisco, at Monte Christi; the Fort of Santa Barbara, at Samana; the Fort of Las Cacoas, at the same place. In addition to this a very limited supply of arms and munitions of war.

The Dominican navy, at the time of my visit, consisted of several schooners, commanded by an admiral.

It struck me that San Domingo, with all her wealth of soil, minerals, and climate, was a hopeless wreck, and would so remain until some power of strength took hold of her and lifted her into a position of reaping the advantage of the elements of prosperity she possessed. She has had her political troubles, brought on only by the imbecile or perverse government of the mother State. This same condition of things was perpetuated for want of sufficient statesmanship among her own people, to establish a firm government. The people, as a class, on the portion of the island I visited, I found harmless, and not naturally disposed to domestic wars, or, in fact, military service, even of any kind. Where they had been called upon, however, to repel invasions, or to overthrow oppression, they had been successful.

In my own mind I was satisfied that a government fairly of the people, with the capacity to summarily quell the disturbances, periodically inaugurated by discontented persons, would be appreciated, and the opening of various industrial pursuits, and inland and ocean commerce, would very soon turn the attention of the masses to more profitable use than ever could be expected under a government constantly trembling in its seat.

I was impressed with the favorable opening the acquisition of the island presented for the establishment of the American doctrine with regard to the territory and States of the western Hemisphere. The geographical position of the island was such as to control the Gulf of Mexico and Caribbean Sea, and the numerous islands to be found in those waters; it had a climate and soil adapted to the completion of our list by adding the productions of the tropics; its people, as far as I could judge, from intercourse with them, were anxious for a change, as their only rescue. That change, they freely admitted, was to link their destiny with the Republic of the United States. With such inducements held out, I thought it not possible that men, professing to be statesmen, would be so short-sighted as to reject any propositions in that direction, should they be made.

I had seen as much of San Domingo as my purposes demanded. My visit to the island was certainly an experience not soon to be forgotten; for the universal hospitality I had received from the people, high and low; for the opportunity of learning something about an island of unparalleled beauty and richness, ruined by the morbid passions of men —an island also possessing an historic interest, dating back to the earliest moments, when a new Hemisphere was born into the world of Civilization and Christianity.

On the 12th of July, the Spanish steamer *Moctezuma*, (Montezuma,) for St. Thomas, was signaled from the top of the ancient tower in which Columbus, over three centuries and a half before, had been in chains. From the same place the caravals of the early explorers were signalled, slowly approaching before the drowsy tropical wind, now steam, the consummation of man's mechanical power, moved a mighty craft against wind and tide.

In the brief space of an hour the steamer dropped anchor, in the roads, off the mouth of the Ozama. From the first movement of the little flag appearing on the signal staff, the city was in a commotion. I at once made my way hastily to the landing. Having here parted with a number of friends, who had come to see me off, I dropped bag and baggage into a clumsy boat, and after a brief pull, found myself on the dirty deck of the *Moctezuma*.

A few hours later, the beautiful shore line of the land of Columbus was fast receding until lost entirely beneath the horizon.

APPENDIX.

Memorandum of Facts relating to the Proposed Annexation of the Island of San Domingo.

In July, 1869, Brevet Brigadier General Orville E. Babcock, of the Corps of Engineers, United States Army, and Secretary to the President of the United States, sailed for San Domingo as the Special Agent of the United States, with reference to certain overtures from the Dominican Government. He carried with him a letter of credence from the President of the United States to Buenaventura Baez, President of the Dominican Republic. He also had written instructions from the State Department, directing him to converse with President Baez upon the subject of the visit. It was stated that the Government had received overtures of annexation, but, according to evidence in the State Department, there existed in San Domingo a difference of opinion on this subject. By some it was thought only a portion of the Government officials were in favor of annexation, but that the President of the Republic was not. General Babcock also received verbal instructions from President Grant, that if he found, on conversation with the President, (Baez,) that this information was correct, that he did not entertain the idea of annexation, he might return, immediately, on the steamer; but if he found he did entertain it, he was to stay over at least one steamer, or, if necessary, longer, and get as much information as he could in reference to the island, in all respects, as to its productions, its fertility, its size, and as to the inclination of the people for annexation.

Senator Cornelius Cole, of California, took passage on the same steamer with General Babcock, but held no official powers.

Arriving at San Domingo City, General Babcock found President Baez at Azua, about one hundred miles east of the capital. He was engaged in matters relating to his army at that point. General Babcock visited President Baez there, but returned immediately to the capital. After an absence of ten days, the President also returned to the capital, when General Babcock commenced the duties which had been laid out for him. The General himself, officially, gives the following narrative of what transpired.

Of President Bacz' views, and what followed, he says, "he was in favor of annexation, and that his Cabinet were with him in favor of it, and he was satisfied that a great majority of his people were in favor of annexation. I told him that I had no authority to make any treaty; that I had only come for matters of information; and I addressed him a memorandum as to points that I should like information upon— the population; the distribution of population; the indebtedness; the nature of the indebtedness; the square miles; a copy of the Constitution; and some other matters of information, which were enumerated in my letter of instructions. I procured, before leaving, answers to all of those points, which, on my return here, I placed on file in the Department. I told President Baez that I had no authority whatever to make a treaty, nor could I bind President Grant in any respect as to a treaty; but I should be very willing to take back any suggestion or any proposition he might have to make to the President of the United States; that I would take it back for his action. I told him that while I could not bind our President, I would give him my opinion of whether it would meet with the approval of President Grant. We were a number of days in the different discussions of these matters of information."

General Babcock remained on the island for forty days, not only in constant conversation with President Baez, but in making some personal observation of the country adjacent to the capital.

Before leaving, a memorandum of points of agreement was prepared and signed by M. M. Gautier, Secretary of State of the Dominican Republic, and General O. E. Babcock, Special Agent of the United States.

General Babcock returned to New York in September, 1869, and at once placed the results of his mission before the President.

On November 10, 1869, General Babcock sailed in the U.

S. Steamer Albany, Captain Balch, from New York for San Domingo, and was accompanied by Colonel and Brevet Major General Delos B. Sackett, Inspector General United States army, and Colonel and Brevet Major General Rufus Ingalls, Assistant Quartermaster General United States army. General Sackett was to act as interpreter, being conversant with the Spanish language, while General Ingalls had a letter from the Secretary of War to accompany General Babcock, and render such assistance as he (Babcock) might wish.

Raymond H. Perry had been appointed Commercial Agent at San Domingo city, and assumed the duties of his office November 16, 1869. He was invested with full and all manner of power and authority, for, and in the name of, the United States, to meet and confer with any person or persons duly authorized by the Government of the Dominican Republic, being invested with like power and authority, and with him or them to agree, treat, consult, and negotiate of and concerning the cession of the dominions and sovereignty of the Dominican Republic to the United States; and also of and concerning a lease to the United States of the portion of such domains contiguous to the Bay of Samana, including the said bay, and all matters and subjects connected therewith; and to conclude and sign a treaty or treaties, convention or conventions, touching the premises, transmitting the same to the President of the United States for his ratification, by and with the advice and consent of the Senate thereof.

Although Mr. Perry was entrusted with the necessary official authority, General Babcock negotiated the treaty, in accordance with detailed instructions from the Government of the United States. General Babcock arrived in San Domingo City on November 18, 1869, and the next day began his negotiations with the Dominican authorities. On November 29, 1869, the treaty was signed by the Dominican government. This document looked to the complete transfer of the jurisdiction of the Island to the United States, in consideration of a stipulated sum. During the same negotiations a lease of the bay and peninsula of Samana was effected. On this a first payment of one hundred and fifty thousand dollars, the annual rental, for a term of fifty years, was paid. In event of the ratification of the treaty of annexation to the United States, the bay and peninsula was to be included, and the lease to be canceled.

General Babcock returned to the United States, and laid the treaty, with accompanying documents, before his Goverment. The treaty was accepted by the Executive, and was sent to the Senate of the United States for ratification. While pending here the complaint of one Davis Hatch was presented, claiming damages against the Dominican government for imprisonment and destruction of property. A special investigation was ordered with reference to this question, and to inquire into certain statements by Perry, who had been commercial agent, and took part in the signing of the treaty. The result of the investigation went to show that Hatch had surrendered his right to American protection, in that he gave aid and comfort to the enemies of the established Dominican government, and that the statements of Perry were without foundation, and, being unsupported by evidence, were unworthy of recognition. The treaty, however, met with great opposition, and, when brought to a vote in the Senate of the United States, in executive session, failed to secure the necessary vote of two-thirds of the Senators present and voting. The treaty was, therefore, rejected.

Previously a movement was started in the lower branch of Congress to effect the acquisition of the island, after the plan adopted in the case of Texas, by joint resolution, in consideration, also, of a certain sum of money. This proposition, however, was not acted upon before the adjournment of Congress, July 15, 1870.

The acquisition of San Domingo would, unquestionably, prove of incalculable benefit to the United States, agriculturally, commercially, and stragetically. As on all former questions of territorial extension, the Executive demonstrated to the country its own wiser statesmanship, as compared with the Senate of the United States. It remains now to be seen whether the United States would follow the provincial diplomatic policy advocated by the Senate, or sustain the broad and comprehensive American doctrine entertained by the Executive.

www.ingramcontent.com/pod-product-compliance
Lightning Source LLC
Chambersburg PA
CBHW021157230426
43667CB00006B/439